ALBUM

BY DAVID RIMMER

★

★

DRAMATISTS
PLAY SERVICE
INC.

ALBUM
Copyright © 1981, David Rimmer
Copyright © 1980, David Rimmer
as an unpublished dramatic composition

All Rights Reserved

SPECIAL NOTE

SPECIAL NOTE ON SONGS AND RECORDINGS

ALBUM was presented by Gene Persson, Richard S. Bright and John Loesser, in association with Twentieth Century-Fox Productions (and by special arrangement with The WPA Theatre), at the Cherry Lane Theatre, in New York City, on October 1, 1980. It was directed by Joan Micklin Silver; the set was by David Potts; costumes were by Susan Denison; the lighting was by Jeff Davis; the sound was by Alex McIntyre; and the production stage manager was Bethe Ward. The cast, in order of appearance, was as follows:

PEGGY . . . . Jenny Wright

TRISH . . . . Jan Leslie Harding

BILLY . . . . Kevin Bacon

BOO . . . . Keith Gordon

SPECIAL NOTE

A special list of revisions and deletions which the author has suggested for high school production of ALBUM appears on page 75 of this acting edition.

CHARACTERS

PEGGY   TRISH   BILLY   BOO

SIDE 1: GIRLS IN BEDROOMS, BOYS IN DORMITORIES

1. **IN MY ROOM**
   October 1963. Trish's bedroom and the hallway outside.
   Night.
   Peggy, Trish, Billy and Boo are 14.

2. **THE LETTER**
   June 1965. Billy's camp. Night.
   Billy is 16.

3. **TICKET TO RIDE**
   August 1965. Trish's bedroom. Dusk.
   Peggy and Trish are 16.

4. **AIN'T IT JUST LIKE THE NIGHT**
   November 1965. Boo's room at school. Twilight.
   Billy and Boo are 16.

SIDE 2: THE NIGHT BEFORE GRADUATION

JUNE 1967

1. **THINGS WE SAID TODAY**
   10 P.M. The High School: the corridors and the
   Teachers' Room.
   Peggy, Billy, Boo and Trish are 18.

2. **BIG GIRLS DON'T CRY**
   Midnight. The Quarry.
   Peggy and Billy.

3. **RUNAWAY**
   2 A.M. A room at the Paradise Motel.
   Trish and Boo.

4. **GRADUATION DAY**
   Dawn. The Quarry.
   Peggy and Billy, Trish and Boo.

6

SET

A small room, three walls, for the bedroom, dorm room, Teachers' Room and motel room scenes. Props and set decorations change with each shift in time period, but the main furniture pieces — window, beds, door, chair — stay the same.

Stage Left and Down Center of the room, a long and narrow playing area for the hallway, letter, corridor and Quarry scenes.

ALBUM

ACT I

1. IN MY ROOM

October 1963. Night. The Beach Boys' "Surfin' U.S.A." is playing. *

Blue spotlight comes up on the hallway D.C., the rest of the set in darkness. Sitting in a circle on the floor, four 14-year old kids, Peggy, Trish, Billy and Boo, are playing strip poker. Trish has much less on than Peggy; Billy and Boo are down to their underwear. Trish is terrified, Peggy supremely confident. Boo loses a hand and takes off his undershirt. Billy deals another hand. Peggy loses and provocatively puts her hand down her blouse and pulls out a hidden necklace. Mad, Billy gives her a dirty look and deals another hand. Trish loses. Billy and Boo look at each other and smile. Trish, panicked, can't figure out what to take off next. Stands up nervously, turns her back. Hesitantly unbuttons her blouse, then desperately looks over to Peggy, who stays cool. Peggy suddenly picks up the cards and throws them in Billy's face. Grabs her clothes and Trish's clothes and they both run up the hall toward the bedroom. Stunned for a second, Billy and Boo then get up and run after them. Lots of noise: shouts, squeals, yelps, screams, hysterical laughter.

The girls run into the bedroom and turn on the light. Peggy locks the door just as Billy and Boo get there. The boys violently pound on the door, yelling and screaming. The girls start putting on their clothes: light-color blouses, plaid just-above-the-knee skirts, or shifts; knee socks, penny loafers; over-sized sweater for Trish, some simple jewelry for Peggy. Peggy's a real beauty, wears her dirty blonde hair long and natural. Cool and knowing, a queen of the school. Trish isn't quite there yet, still awkward and self-conscious and itchy, the fact that she's a girl almost hidden. Her hair is medium-short and indecisive.

*See Special Note on copyright page

9

Her bedroom has two identical beds coming out from the U. wall; between them, a manual record player, a couple of Beach Boys albums, lots of 45's; soft chair; door U.C. Small magazine pictures of the Beach Boys on the wall, books, notebooks, trinkets, clothes, toy animals all around the room. Window on Right wall: blue moonlight shining through, stars and trees outside.

Peggy moves to the door, enjoying her triumph. Music fades down and out. Trish stands in one spot, frozen with fear, muttering and chanting.

TRISH. I can't do this. . . Peggy. . . I can't do this. . .

PEGGY. (*Teasing the boys.*) And don't come in 'til we're dressed! You're lucky if we letcha in at all! You cheat, Billy! (*To Trish.*) —He always puts a coupla aces in his underpants—

BILLY. (*To Boo: mad and frustrated.*) She always accuses me of cheatin'!

BOO. You *were* cheatin'.

BILLY. *So?* (*Billy gives Boo a "How can you be so dumb?" look, pounds violently on the door. Trish jumps a mile.*)

PEGGY. Forget it, Billy!

BILLY. Aah, whadda we care?

BOO. (*Shocked.*) *What?*

BILLY. *Whadda we care?*

BOO. Whaddayou sayin'?

BILLY. Whadda we care.

TRISH. I can't do this. . . I can't do this. . .

BOO. (*Desperate.*) Don'tcha wanna get in there?

BILLY. (*Blowing up.*) OH JEEZ!! All right—look! (*Billy takes a running start. Peggy motions Trish to shut up, then goes and listens, her ear at the door. Billy slams into the door with a loud crash.*) Eeeennn-nyyyyowwww . . . *PT 109*!! . . . . . pschhhhhhh! ! ! !

PEGGY. You're *never* gettin' in now!

BOO. (*To Billy.*) Nice goin'.

PEGGY. (*Quickly opening the door and scolding him like a little kid; shutting it just as quick.*) You put your pants back on, Boo Piercy! (*Boo, surprised and humiliated, slinks D. with his clothes, sits meekly. Billy, seething with anger, sits too, rubbing a sore arm. They both start dressing: button-down or snap-tab collars on madras or pin-striped shirts; chino or continental pants; shoes, black or brown non-penny loafers; white socks. Billy is tall, good-looking; athletic body, cool guy. Boo is little, skinny, barely on the periphery of coolness; gets by with his weird sense of humor. Billy nurses his anger, Boo sits tight and scared. Hallway lights fade out. Trish unfreezes, starts pacing nervously.*) Show them — What's the matter?

TRISH. I can't do this —

PEGGY. Well you're doin' it, so shut up.

TRISH. It felt weird playin' so near my parents' bedroom —

PEGGY. — They won't come back —

TRISH. — I know —

PEGGY. You gotta do it sometime. You're 14 years old! You wanna wait 'til you're an old maid — ?

TRISH. No —

PEGGY. Don't you like boys?

TRISH. Yeah —

PEGGY. Whaddaya gonna do, wear a "KEEP OFF — NO TRESPASSING" sign on you your whole life?

TRISH. *No!* I want them to trespass on me! It isn't that —

PEGGY. *What?*

TRISH. Nothin'. There's just somethin' wrong with me, okay? This room's so small.

PEGGY. Don'tya ever think about boys?

TRISH. (*Exasperated.*) *I think about them all the time!*

PEGGY. Okay, there's two of 'em out there right now, so what's the — (*Peggy leaps from one bed to the other, where Trish is sitting.*)

TRISH. (*Exploding.*) It's not boys like Boo, or Billy, I think about! I don't lie in bed at night and have dreams about them the way I do about Brian — (*Didn't mean to let it slip out.*) — Uh-oh.

PEGGY. Brian?

TRISH. Never mind.

PEGGY. Who's Brian?

TRISH. *Shut up!*

PEGGY. Who's Brian?

TRISH. (*Shamed.*) Wilson. In the Beach Boys. I have dreams about him.

PEGGY. Brian? The tall one?

TRISH. They're not regular dreams —

PEGGY. I like the blonde one, Dennis? The drummer? He's cute —

TRISH. (*Crazy desperate.*) Shut up!! I'm in love with Brian Wilson! Don't you understand? I love him! I have weird thoughts about him! I could never do anything sexy with a regular boy —

11

PEGGY. Hey, what's wrong with you? Everybody likes the Beach Boys—

TRISH. *It's not like everybody!* Leave me alone, I wanna go home—

PEGGY. You *are* home—

TRISH. —oh—

PEGGY. —Dufus. What's the big deal? Tons of girls like the Beach Boys—

TRISH. *It's not like tons of girls!* It's not normal, it's not the way other girls feel, I know it—

PEGGY. It is so normal—

TRISH. You call this normal? (*She reaches under her bed and takes out an old photograph album.*)

BILLY. (*Bellowing.*) —HEY GIRL—

PEGGY. —*Suffer!*— What?

TRISH. It's this picture album we've had in our family a million centuries. My mother passed it down to me the day I entered womanhood. Lookit. That's where I wrote out all the words to "A Thousand Stars in the Sky" by Kathy Young and the Innocents cause it was the first song I ever bought and my mother yelled at me to turn it off after I played it 65 times. (*Melodramatic.*) That's how I started.

PEGGY. Started what?

TRISH. See those little pictures of my granma and my granpa at their wedding? (*Almost in tears.*) You can hardly see my granma's face cause I wrote the words to "Surfer Girl" over her. I'm sick. Look. All the words to all the Beach Boys songs, cause Brian writes all the songs. Pictures of them, pictures of Brian— (*Peggy tries to take a closer look, but Trish yanks the album away.*) —And you should see the dreams I have! Talk about *sick*—

PEGGY. You're not sick.

TRISH. I'm not normal.

PEGGY. Don't say that.

TRISH. I'm not normal.

PEGGY. That's not true.

TRISH. I'm not normal.

PEGGY. SHUT UP!! You're normal!

TRISH. If I was normal, I wouldn't go around saying "I'm not normal, I'm not normal" like that. (*She turns and looks out the window.*) Star light star bright first star I see tonight. . .

PEGGY. Earth to Trish, Earth to Trish. . .

TRISH. (*Whirls around; rapid-fire.*) Wish I may wish I might have the wish I wish tonight.

PEGGY. You're not normal. (*Lights fade out on the bedroom, come up on the hall where the boys are finished dressing. Trish sits in the chair, curled up, withdrawn. Peggy ignores her, begins writing her name in her notebook a million times. Billy, sulking, gets up suddenly, angrily.*)

BILLY. I'm sick of this!

BOO. (*Anxious.*) We're not gonna leave, are we?

BILLY. (*Softening; smiling.*) You retard. You like Trish?

BOO. Yeah. I was lookin' through her stuff when you guys were gettin' the cards. She's got this picture album with all these old pictures in it, but she covered 'em up with pictures of the Beach Boys. And she's got the words to their songs written on 'em.

BILLY. (*Man of the world.*) I've seen girls do weirder stuff than that.

BOO. What's weird about it? (*Billy smacks him.*) Bet she uses those pictures to get hot over.

BILLY. That's stupid. Gettin' hot over somebody you'll never get close to in a million years.

BOO. What's stupid about it? (*Another smack.*) Don't you like Marilyn Monroe?

BILLY. She's dead, ya twink.

BOO. What about Mrs. Kennedy?

BILLY. Jackie?

BOO. Yeah! What a piece —

BILLY. You're sick! (*As Billy and Boo scuffle, playfully exchanging slaps and body blocks, Trish gets up, and with a defiant look over to Peggy, goes to the record player and puts on a 45: "Be True to Your School," the Beach Boys.* Peggy looks up a second, then chooses to ignore her. Billy stops fighting and listens, unconsciously moving to the music. Boo does the same thing, also mouthing the lyrics. Billy sees him, remembers that he's mad.*) I don't believe this! They're playin' records now!

BOO. (*Nervously sneaking glances at the agitated Billy.*) Too bad we don't have a school decent enough to be true to. Martin Van Buren High. We can't even get a decent guy to get named after. We should call it somethin' else. . .

BILLY. (*Bursts out.*) Will you shut up? (*Yells at the door.*) They better let us in sometime tonight, we got school tomorrow!

BOO. (*Copying him.*) Yeah!

*See Special Note on copyright page

13

PEGGY. Stay out there and suffer, you dinks!

BOO. Oh jeez. . . (*Tugs at Billy's sleeve.*) Think I got a chance with Trish tonight?

BILLY. What? Make out?

BOO. Yeah. Think she puts out? (*Billy shrugs.*) Maybe I should join the Beach Boys. You really think she's weird?

BILLY. I dunno, maybe she thinks I'm weird.

BOO. I think she thinks you're conceited.

BILLY. (*Stops; slowly, slowly turns his head.*) *What?*

BOO. Yeah. Y'know what I mean?

BILLY. I'm not conceited.

BOO. *I* know. But I think *she* thinks you are. Y'know what I mean?

BILLY. *I'm not conceited.*

BOO. I *know!*

BILLY. *What makes her think I'm conceited?*

BOO. I DON'T KNOW! Just seems that way.

BILLY. (*Pacing, muttering, brooding.*) Just seems that way. Well, I don't think she thinks I'm conceited. Besides, I'm not. Conceited. Peggy doesn't think I'm conceited.

BOO. That's true. (*Beat.*) Peggy already knows you're a dink.

BILLY. Funny. Y'know we took her to that party at Timmy Trumbull's Friday night? Peggy said it was so she could meet some guys. 'Cept the whole time we were there, she didn't say a word hardly. She just sat on this one couch by herself the whole night, with this weird look on her face, holdin' this bottle of Seven-Up. She already drank it and everything, it was empty, but she kept holdin' it the whole time. (*Billy, getting impatient at Boo not understanding him, finally just belts him.*)

BOO. You missed a great *Twilight Zone.*

BILLY. Yeah? Friday?

BOO. That's who we should name our school after! Rod Serling High School. (*Rod Serling imitation.*) If you sign that lavatory pass, you could be taking a one-way trip into. . . The Twilight Zone.

BILLY. (*Laughing.*) Shut up, what was it?

BOO. It was great. This real creepy guy gets this stopwatch that's magic or somethin! Whenever he clicks it. . . Time stops. The whole world's frozen, everybody right where they were, everybody except him. He can walk around and do anything. Rob banks, steal food. . . I'd give anything to have one of those. Feel up any girl you want.

BILLY. What?
BOO. (*Sensually lying on his stomach.*) They'd be frozen, they wouldn't even know. You could do anything to 'em. Feel their tits, their legs. . .
BILLY. What're you talkin' about?
BOO. Nothin' —
BILLY. That's disgusting!
BOO. — or you could be invisible and knock 'em unconscious. . .
BILLY. *That's even worse*!! I don't know how you expect girls to — I never should've done this! Next time you get girls on your own — (*Boo turns away, hurt. After a minute, Billy relents, and crosses to him.*) Here, take this. (*Gives him a stick of gum. Boo chews it hungrily.*) Now just shape up. We'll wait for 'em a little while more, okay? Whaddaya wanna do? Pitch pennies?
BOO. Naw. There's one Penny I'd like to pitch, boy. Penny Pounder. You know that new girl? Whaddaya think?
BILLY. She's a *seventh-grader*, for God's sake!
BOO. So? I like 'em young. (*Billy gives him a disgusted look, trying to be tough. They stare at each other. As the hall lights fade, Boo gives him a crazy smile. Billy begins to smile too. Lights crossfade back to the bedroom. Agitated, Trish gets up and goes over to the record player, carrying the photograph album with her. She looks over to Peggy, who continues to ignore her. She starts to take the 45 off, then, angry and frustrated, throws the album down and yells to Peggy.*)
TRISH. You know what else? You know that party we went to Friday night, that you and Billy *took* me to, at Timmy what's-his-name's house?
PEGGY. We didn't *take* you, you just came with us, that's all —
TRISH. What's the difference? Soon as we got there you guys started dancin', so I was lookin' around and. . .
PEGGY. Well maybe somebody woulda asked you to dance if you weren't carryin' around that stupid bottle of Seven-Up all night —
TRISH. *Peggy!*
PEGGY. *Okay.*
TRISH. (*Anger and desperation building.*) And I noticed Joanne Glorioso and Johnny Noonan. They were in that corner, they were making out for the whole party practically, they hardly ever stopped. I've never seen anybody making out so much, and so *fast*. But I could never do that with a boy. Not like that, so fast and scary. It made me feel creepy, but I kept turning back and

15

watchin' them, I couldn't help it, and I kept thinking about Brian, I kept seeing his face. I tried to stop but I couldn't. I closed my eyes but he was still there. All these things were goin' round in my head, it felt — I thought I was going crazy! I've never made out with anybody and I never will! I know it! I'm too crazy! *I'm crazy!*

PEGGY. (*Coming over to comfort her.*) Yes you will, it's all right —

TRISH. (*Pulling away. Anger reaching a furious peak.*) Yeah, Peggy. "It's all right." You can say that, it's easy for you. You got Billy, you got all the boys in the school comin' up to you all the time. You're normal. Don't have creepy feelings, creepy dreams — lie in bed and can't sleep cause you keep seeing things — kissing boys you'll never get to kiss — and touching — and — *you're not a psycho!* (*Grabs a stuffed animal and throws it.*)

PEGGY. Hey. . .

TRISH. (*Suddenly quiet and timid.*) I'm sorry — (*Flops down on the bed, hiding her face.*)

PEGGY. It's okay.

TRISH. There's somethin' weird about me. . .

PEGGY. (*Sits next to her.*) It's not just you. I have funny feelings too, everything isn't great for me all the time. (*Making a declaration.*) Billy and me aren't in love.

TRISH. You don't love Billy?

PEGGY. First time I ever danced with Billy, he was shakin' all around like a washing machine. I couldn't believe it. . . And I have creepy dreams all the time.

TRISH. Tell me one.

PEGGY. I don't wanna tell any stupid dream.

TRISH. I told you all that stuff!

PEGGY. So? (*Trish just looks at her.*) Okay. This one I had, I was coming back into my room after school, and I saw Billy sittin' at my make-up table, lookin' into the mirror, all dressed up like a girl. He had my yellow blouse on and my pin and my skirt and he was puttin' make-up on. I was so mad, I threw my books on the floor and I started yellin' at him, but the words I was saying didn't make any sense. Then he got this real funny look on his face and he got up and he said in this weird English accent, "This isn't my cup of tea, is it?" And he walked out the door, and I was just standin' there, feelin' really really stupid. Then I woke up. Think that's normal?

TRISH. No. . .

16

PEGGY. Okay, it's not just you. And lots of times when me and Billy're kissin', I start thinkin' about . . . seein'. . . other things.
TRISH. Really? How do you know you're not crazy?
PEGGY. Maybe I am.
TRISH. Does everybody do that?
PEGGY. Everybody.
TRISH. Everybody isn't crazy. . . (*She cuddles up to Peggy, who strokes her hair. Lights slowly fade. Then come up on the hallway. Billy is pacing, Boo sitting on the floor way D., mumbling, curled into a scrunched-up ball.*)
BOO. . . .jeez . . . wish I . . . Oh . . . God . . . gotta get — whoa . . . give anything for a feel right now. . .
BILLY. (*Coming D.*) Hey . . . slow down.
BOO. I'm shakin' inside.
BILLY. It's all right.
BOO. All right for you. You've done this.
BILLY. Take it easy.
BOO. (*Chanting almost.*) Yeah, I know. . . Take it easy. Take it slow. Don't rush. Don't let 'em know you're thinkin' about it. Slow and easy. Nice and slow. I know. . . I know. . . (*Gets up.*) How we gonna get 'em to let us in? (*Billy crosses to the door, starts to knock, but changes his mind. Makes a move to go.*)
BILLY. I'm leavin'.
BOO. Billy!
BILLY. I can't wait around for her all night.
BOO. (*Panic.*) Well — whereya goin'?
BILLY. They're all the same in the dark.
BOO. Whaddaya mean?
BILLY. Plenty of girls around here won't keep me waitin'.
BOO. Thanks.
BILLY. Hey . . . what?
BOO. What'm I supposed to do here by myself?
BILLY. You can come with me.
BOO. What, to other girls' houses, watch you make out?
BILLY. No, I — I'm not really gonna do that — *I just can't sit around and wait for Peggy all night!*
BOO. I'm never gonna get to make out.
BILLY. Look, I ain't gonna either.
BOO. You know what I mean by "never"? (*They look at each other. Lights crossfade to the bedroom. Trish is lying on the bed, Peggy sitting next to her.*)

17

TRISH. It's always right before I go to sleep. I take my radio from under the pillow, and I put it away, and I lie there and close my eyes. . . Sorta like dreaming but I'm awake too. . . We're walking on the beach, me and Brian, not holding hands or anything, just walking. The sun's going down over the ocean, there's nobody else there, you can hear the waves. Then we stop, right at the edge. I look at his face, and I know he's gonna touch me, I can feel it, like a fire. I look at the sky behind him and I can see the stars, I can count them, it's not even dark. Then he says, "Listen. . . " And I close my eyes, and I hear the ocean, and I feel it inside me, tingling, and warm, and I can't wait for him to touch me. . . The beach is in California. Can you imagine? The Pacific Ocean. . . I can't even think of it, it's so far. Think we'll ever get to go there, Peg? I'd give anything to go. . . (*Beat. Hall lights on. Boo counts off, "One, two, three," and at the door, he and Billy start singing the Beach Boys' "Little Deuce Coupe."** Peggy leaps up, all business and action. The boys continue with the rest of the song, giggling, hamming it up, shoving each other around, as the girls shout to be heard over them.*)
PEGGY. I forgot they were there! C'mon!
TRISH. (*Panic.*) What?
PEGGY. Get ready. (*Shouts.*) Hold it you guys, we'll be ready in a minute! (*Grabs Trish, pulls her over to the mirror.*)
TRISH. (*Resisting.*) Whaddayou doin'?
PEGGY. Gonna get you some boys.
TRISH. But I told you! I can't! I don't wanna—!
PEGGY. I don't care! C'mere, lemme see your face.
TRISH. Peggy—!
PEGGY. Do what I tell ya! (*Still singing, the boys pound on the door, getting wilder. Peggy looks Trish over.*) That's good enough. C'mon.
TRISH. I can't!
PEGGY. You can so!
TRISH. But not with Boo— He's not my kind of guy—
PEGGY. —Don't worry about it!—
TRISH. —I don't know what to do!— I can't think—
PEGGY. —Don't think about it!—
TRISH. —But I don't know how!—
PEGGY. Shut up! (*To the boys.*) All right, all right! (*Just about to open the door, she takes a quick look back over the room.*) Hide this! Hide

18

it' Quick! (*Trish hides the picture album.*) Hurry up! (*Peggy opens the door. Trish freezes. The boys control their outburst and step in, shyly, coolly, hands in their pockets, Billy first, Boo hanging back.*)

BILLY. Hey.

PEGGY. Hi.

BILLY. What took ya so long?

PEGGY. Trish wasn't feelin' good for a while but she's okay now.

BILLY. Hey Trish.

TRISH. Hi.

BOO. Howdy.

PEGGY. (*Sarcastic.*) You guys are great singers.

BILLY. We figured you'd like it.

BOO. (*To Trish.*) We figured since you're the world's greatest Beach Boys fan —

BILLY. We figured we'd serenade ya.

PEGGY. Well, you figured right for a change. But you're still dumb.

BILLY. Hey girl —

PEGGY. Don't "Hey girl" me. Anybody who goes around cheatin' at strip poker —

BILLY. I wasn't cheatin', don't start that again —

PEGGY. Boo? Was he cheatin'? You tell me. He was, wasn't he?

BOO. I dunno — I —

PEGGY. Well never mind. I don't want to know. I want you to dance with me.

BOO. What?

BILLY. What is this —

PEGGY. I'm not dancin' with any strip poker cheater. Trish. (*She punches Billy, grabs Trish and drags her over to him.*) You're too good for him, but I don't wantcha to feel left out when me and Marston start steppin' out.

BOO. How'd you know my name?

PEGGY. Never you mind. I have my ways. (*She sprawls across the bed and picks out a 45.*)

BILLY. What's goin' on?

PEGGY. You shut up.

TRISH. Peggy —

PEGGY. You shut up too. (*About to play the record. Really fast.*) This is dedicated to Trish and while it's playin' she can close her eyes and see whatever she wants.

BILLY. What? ("Surfer Girl," the Beach Boys, plays.* Peggy yanks Trish and Billy together.)

PEGGY. Dance. (They begin to dance, hesitantly, between the beds. Peggy turns off a lamp. Lighting is moonlight, soft blue, romantic.) Atmosphere. (Boo whispers to Billy, as Peggy pulls him into a dancing position.)

BOO. What's goin' on?

PEGGY. C'mon Marston, I wanna dance.

BOO. How'd you know my real name?

PEGGY. What's the matter? I think it's a nice name.

BOO. Y'do?

PEGGY. Yeah, now shhhh. (She pulls him closer to her and they dance. Billy and Trish dance closer; he holds her hand under his chin.) C'mere Marston. I wanna sit on your lap. (She leads him to the chair, Boo delirious and happy and completely mystified. Peggy plays with his face and his hair, and soon they start kissing, shyly at first, then more passionate. Billy sees them. Then Billy and Trish go into a long hard kiss, still dancing. Peggy, to Boo, softly, between kisses.) Let's switch our gum. (Boo laughs numbly, agreeable to anything. They kiss some more, switching gum. Billy and Trish ease down to sit on the bed, never taking their mouths from each other. After a while, Peggy stops and looks over to them. They're all in a golden haze, their voices husky and breathy.) What's goin' on over there?

BOO. (Sings.) Yeah. . . Hey Billy. . . Do you love me . . . Surfer Girl. . .*

BILLY. Hey. (To Peggy.) Kid thinks he's a singer.

PEGGY. Whaddayou know?

BILLY. Plenty.

PEGGY. They're all the same in the dark? You barely know how to kiss. (Billy shoots her an angry look, then gives Trish a big sweeping romantic kiss. Boo and Peggy go back to making out. After a minute, Trish, barely able to breathe, stops the kiss.)

TRISH. Peggy, I know what you mean, everything's okay, I think it's okay —

PEGGY. Shh. Don't think. (They all go back to making out as the next record flips over and plays: "In My Room," the Beach Boys.)*

SLOW FADE TO BLACK

*See Special Note on copyright page

20

ACT I

2. THE LETTER

June 1965. Billy's camp. Night. Lighting: moonlight and the wavy blue reflection of it on a lake. Sound: crickets. Billy, 16, sits in the D.C. area, flashing a flashlight, looking around. He reads from a piece of paper, a spotlight isolating him, the rest of the set in darkness. He's wearing summer clothes: cutoff shorts, sweatshirt, barefoot, a pencil in his hand.

BILLY. Dear Marston,
You incredible dipshit, what'm I doin' wastin' my time writin' a letter to you? Bein' a junior counsellor sucks. I hate tellin' kids what to do. They have to call me "Mister." I wake up in the mornin', they go, "Hey, Mister Buddwing, I wet my bed," and I think, "No, sorry, my father isn't here right now."
One cool thing. We had a party with the girl counsellors at this place Camp Idle Pines for Girls across the lake. We bought some beer. That's the other cool thing. The older guys go into town and get it for you. Anyway, I got some great action at that party. Y'know that album *The Beach Boys Today?* Cool album for parties. They put all the fast songs on the first side and all the slow songs on the second side, y'know, for dancin' and then makin' out. Really a cool idea. The Beatles oughtta do somethin' like that. Course it doesn't matter, everybody buys their records anyway — (*Crosses it out.*) — God, who gives a shit about that? — So I end up with this girl Rita, and she's not exactly slutty or anything, but she's kinda fast. We're goin' at it, and they put on side two of that album. On "Please Let Me Wonder," we're dancin' close — very close; on "I'm So Young," squeezin' legs; on "Kiss Me Baby," lickin' ears; on "She Knows Me Too Well," swappin' spit; and by the time we hit "Way In The Back Of My Mind," my tongue was so Way In The Back of Her Head we didn't even *hear* the rest of the shit on the album! Woo! (*Fearing he's too loud, he looks around, flashing the flashlight.*) So that's how it is up here, you turd-ball,

21

'cept I'm lyin' just a little to show you how cool I am. Aaah, I'm wastin' my time. You stupid asshole, what the hell you doin' goin' away to school way up in the goddamn woods? Go ahead, I'm not gonna stop ya, whadda I care, I'm not gonna miss ya, that ain't cool. Get on up there. See ya sometime.
Sincerely yours, you dipshit,
Signed, Billy Bones
P.S. Have a good life.
                              (*Beat.*)
What a bunch of shit. (*Crumples the paper, throws it down.*)

                              BLACKOUT

ACT I

3. TICKET TO RIDE

August 1965. Trish's room. Dusk. The Beatles' "Ticket to Ride" plays loud. *

Lights up: the bedroom is barer than before, not as much junk all over the place. Beach Boys pictures on the wall now replaced by Beatles pictures, still small, magazine-style; a new princess phone, red. Outside the window: the last moments of a beautiful sunset coming through the trees.

Trish, 16, is sprawled on the floor Downstage, one hand holding up a picture of John Lennon, as she gazes at it, a transistor radio next to her, blaring. She's wearing summer clothes, shorts and a sleeveless blouse; her body is beginning to fill out, she's looking more like a girl; her hair a little longer, more in control, her face less hidden. She listens to an Offstage voice and reluctantly responds to it.

TRISH. *Okay! Okay! (She grudgingly turns down the radio, and the volume of "Ticket to Ride" goes down. She gets up, muttering and grumbling as she walks around the room in frustration.)* Haven't you gone yet?. . . God. . . *(She looks out the window and hears the sound of a car starting up and pulling away. She yells.)* I'll listen as loud as I want! *(Afraid she said it too loud, she takes a quick look outside, then, relieved, goes to her radio, and turns it back up. She sings along with the second verse of the song, changing the lyrics to show her anger toward her parents: from "She" and "me" to "I" and "you."* As she sings, she takes out her mother's picture album and a pen, and a pack of cigarettes with matches and ashtray — all hidden under the bed. She sits on the floor and defiantly lights a cigarette. After a second or two of pleasure, the smoke gets in her eyes, and she reacts in pain. Then she turns her attention to the album, leafing through it, writing in it, turning down the radio a bit.)* Writin' in your sacred old picture album again, Mom. "A Thousand Stars," "Surfer Girl."

*See Special Note on copyright page

Ecch. Ancient history. (*Smiles.*) "Eight Days A Week," "Help!" "Ticket To Ride." Here's what happens, Mom: I meet John Lennon at a party and he needs help just like a regular person, he's having problems with Cynthia and he's just waiting for the right bird to fly away with and I'm it and we run away together and leave you and your old album behind. And he's my Ticket to Ride. . . (*She kisses the picture of John on the lips; then gets up.*) Sick. Gotta stop fallin' in love with pictures. (*Looks out the window.*) C'mon, get dark. (*The sound of a car pulling into the driveway scares her. She fans the air for smoke, hides the cigarettes, runs to the window.*) Shit! Back already? Can't you give me any peace—? (*Yelps in delight.*) Peggy! (*Looks closer.*) Barb? And a guy—? (*She runs out the door as the radio plays, and after a second or two, she and Peggy, 16 too, rush back into the room. Peggy is wearing summer clothes, looks great in them. She seems the same, maybe a little more cynical and bored; no cracks in her front yet. They're playfully arguing, giggling like crazy, words overlapping, as they run to the window, music slowly fading down and out.*)
PEGGY. —I had the worst summer of all time—
TRISH. —No, I had the worst summer of all time—
PEGGY. —No, I did— *Wait!* What's Barb doin'?
TRISH. Who's that guy, he looks so hoody— Move!
PEGGY. —I can't see! God, I can't believe she's gonna do it with him—
TRISH. Do what?
PEGGY. It.
TRISH. *It?* You mean— How do you know? How can you tell?
PEGGY. She told me.
TRISH. Oh.
PEGGY. Wait! He's bending down! Look!
TRISH. Oh my God, he's goin' for it already! (*Sound of car engine gunning.*)
PEGGY. Nah, he's just revvin' it up. What a grub. Rory. (*They both giggle.*) She could've picked a guy with a better name.
TRISH. And one that didn't look like he just got out of state prison. (*Sound of the car pulling away; they watch it drive out of sight.*)
PEGGY. She said to stay here and wait for her 'til she gets back. Then she'll tell us all about it.
TRISH. God, you go away for a summer and look what happens. You didn't do it too, didya?
PEGGY. Wanna hear somethin' sad? Midnight died—

TRISH. Your cat?

PEGGY. He got hit by a car. Splat. (*Peggy starts checking out the room.*) Oh my God, you got your own phone now? (*Picks up the receiver, speaks into it.*) Princess. (*Sits on the bed, looks into the album.*) And still gettin' hot over pictures. . . ?

TRISH. Shut up! What about Barb?

PEGGY. What about her?

TRISH. The first time you do it, it hurts, doesn't it? And it bleeds?

PEGGY. I guess.

TRISH. (*Wondrous.*) But only for a second. Then every time afterwards it doesn't. . . Hey—

PEGGY. What?

TRISH. Do you think—no—

PEGGY. *What?*

TRISH. You think you'd— Think you'd ever do it with one of the Beatles?

PEGGY. *Dugan!*— God!—

TRISH. —If you had the chance—

PEGGY. I don't know—

TRISH. —Would you?—

PEGGY. —Cut it out—

TRISH. —*Come on*, would you?—

PEGGY. —All right, yeah, I guess so—

TRISH. Which one?

PEGGY. Dugan, gimme a break. Haven't you gotten over the Beatles yet?

TRISH. —I'll never get over them—

PEGGY. (*Leafing through album.*) I remember when it was Brian Wilson and the Beach Boys.

TRISH. Bullshit.

PEGGY. You kiss your mother with that mouth?

TRISH. (*Sighs.*) I've never even seen a boy's, you know.

PEGGY. I saw my brother's in the bathtub once. (*They both giggle.*)

TRISH. Really? What'd it look like?

PEGGY. Like a mushroom. With a little eye at the end of it. Then when it gets big, it's like a mushroom on top of a rocket.

TRISH. It gets big? I thought it just, you know, stood up. Like an erection. (*Hesitant pause.*) Do you know, um, do the balls go in with it or do they stay outside?

25

PEGGY. (*Embarrassed.*) Gross! —

TRISH. My mother never told me anything she was supposed to. She said stuff like, "A kiss should end the evening, not begin it." And "Why buy a cow when you can already taste the milk?"

PEGGY. What does that mean?

TRISH. Don't do it before you're married.

PEGGY. Vomitous.

TRISH. I wonder if Barb'll have to get married.

PEGGY. *Will you shut up about Barb?*

TRISH. What's the matter? You did it too, didn't you?

PEGGY. No, I— Never mind.

TRISH. Some friend. You and Barb go off and do it and leave me— (*Stops and stares at Peggy.*)

PEGGY. What're you doin'?

TRISH. Tryin' to see if you look different.

PEGGY. What?

TRISH. You look different after you do it. That's what happens.

PEGGY. How can you look different?

TRISH. I don't know! You turn into a woman and you look different. Don't ask me. (*Beat.*) You look the same to me. Didya feel different after you did it?

PEGGY. *Will you leave me alone?*

TRISH. What's the matter?

PEGGY. No— I— did— not— feel— different.

TRISH. Why not?

PEGGY. *Dugan!*

TRISH. Peggy. . . What—? Aren't you gonna tell me about it?

PEGGY. Why?

TRISH. Cause you're my friend, that's why.

PEGGY. Why don't you just wait for Barb to get back. She's your friend too.

TRISH. Cause— She's not my friend the way you are. Okay? *Cause I want you to tell me!* (*Peggy smiles, drifts off for a second, glances at some of Trish's old toys.*)

PEGGY. Remember that time when we were little kids and we became blood sisters?

TRISH. Yeah, and the knife slipped and I got an infection. I still got the scar.

PEGGY. Lemme see. (*Trish holds out her hand. Peggy takes it in hers, holds it, then bites it. Trish cries "Ow!", backs away, her hand at her mouth, sucking at the sore.*)

TRISH. You're weird. God, if it changes you this much, I don't know if I wanna do it.

PEGGY. (*Coming over to her.*) I'm sorry! I'm sorry, I just wanted to be blood sisters again. (*She takes Trish's hand and gently kisses it on the sore spot and then walks away. Amazed, Trish just stares at her.*) I met this guy from another town. I didn't even know his name.

TRISH. God. . .

PEGGY. Shh— Don't talk. (*Beat.*) I drove down to the Quarry with him, and we parked the car. (*Trish sits down, listening, all rapt attention.*) There wasn't anybody else there. There was a full moon, I could see it through the windshield. We got in the back seat . . . 1st Base, 2nd Base, 3rd Base. . . He kept touching me down there. You remember the first time you felt . . . you got wet?

TRISH. Tell me about now.

PEGGY. First time it happened to me was way back with Billy. That was nice. (*Looks at Trish, who's still anxiously waiting.*) Okay, we're in the back seat, and practically all our clothes are off. Then he goes and gets a rubber. Eeuu. And he gets on top of me and starts moanin' and groanin' like he was dyin' or something. Then I feel something touching me down there and I think, "Okay, okay, it's only gonna hurt a second." But it keeps hurting, and it isn't going in. I said, "What's the matter?" And he said, "No, it's okay, it's okay." He wanted me to put my hand on it. It was all slimy. And he keeps trying and trying and it still won't go in. He was sweating on me. I felt so squished. I pushed him off me, and he was just sitting there with this stupid look on his face, and I thought, "This is it?" So I said to him, "There's something wrong with one of us." He didn't say anything.

TRISH. (*Her face fallen.*) That isn't true.

PEGGY. I'm never doin' it again. First and last.

TRISH. (*Can't believe it.*) That happened to *you?*

PEGGY. No, it happened to Shelley Fabares. (*Trish just stares at Peggy, who keeps her face turned away. Pause. The phone rings. Trish, never taking her eyes off Peggy, answers it.*)

TRISH. Hello?. . . Barb?. . . What—? (*Listens.*) . . .God. . . Yeah, where are ya?. . . Okay, we'll be right there. . . I promise.. . Just keep listenin' to your radio, okay?. . . What—? They played "Satisfaction" and now they're playin' "Wooly Bully"? Great. Okay, we're comin'. Bye. (*Hangs up. Stands there stunned.*) She started doin' it with the guy, and he asked if she was a virgin

27

or not. She said yeah, he said forget it, and he kicked her out of the car and left her on the beach.

PEGGY. Figures.

TRISH. How're you supposed to get to *not* be a virgin?

(Trish stands still, not sure what to do. Peggy lies down on the bed and looks at Trish's pictures. Trish puts her sandals on, then turns back to Peggy.) Come on. . . We better go. . .

PEGGY. Maybe it's better with pictures. *(Trish yanks Peggy up and they both go out the door, arms around each other.)*

BLACKOUT

ACT I

4. AIN'T IT JUST LIKE THE NIGHT

November 1965. Bob Dylan's "Positively 4th Street" plays. * *Boo's room at school. Twilight. Out the window: bare trees and the outlines of buildings.*

Two beds in the room, two of everything. The room is crowded, cramped, all the furniture so close together there's barely walking space. Clothes, records, sports equipment, books, record player. The main decoration is a blanket hung on the wall with dozens of magazine photos of women in bathing suits, scanty gowns: Ursula Andress, Claudia Cardinale, Elke Sommer, Lee Remick, several Life magazine shots of Jackie Kennedy living it up in Spain. All women; no pictures or posters of Bob Dylan.

Lights up: Boo is sitting on D. chair near record player, listening intensely to "Positively 4th Street," moving with the music, singing along, playing an imaginary electric organ. Billy is lying on U. bed, bored, idly playing with a football. Billy stays cool most of the time. Boo is fast-talking, fidgets a lot. Clothes: pin-striped or light blue shirts; corduroy pants; tie for Billy, loose; no shoes for Boo, desert boots for Billy; dark socks for both. They're 16.

The song ends. Boo jumps up.

BOO. See? What'd I tell ya? Greatest song of all time.
BILLY. (*Holding back.*) It's all right.
BOO. It's all right? That's the greatest song I ever heard in my life. It's all right. (*Dylan voice.*) Such an incredible drag for me to see you. (*Billy just sits there smiling; the hand behind his head shoots out the finger.*) He's greater than the Beatles.
BILLY. How can he be greater than the Beatles? They're four guys. That's stupid.

*See Special Note on copyright page

BOO. (*Dylan voice.*) Got some kinda nerve sayin' you're my friend.

BILLY. (*Acting tough.*) Oh yeah? Who said I was?

BOO. You. (*Beat.*) 'Bout time this song came out up here. Takes everything ten years to get here. (*Dylan.*) This place's so slow, it's invisible. — I can't believe you didn't like that song.

BILLY. What song?

BOO. Aarrhh! I'm gonna kill you!

BILLY. (*Jumps off the bed; fists up.*) Put up your dukes.

BOO. (*Beginning to laugh.*) Wh — ? Put up my dukes?. . . That's stupid — (*Both of them jockeying around each other like fighters in the ring, giggling.*)

BILLY. What's stupid?

BOO. You're stupid —

BILLY. — Oh yeah? —

BOO. You're brain-damaged —

BILLY. Where ya think I got it from? Hangin' around spastics like you —

BOO. Ahh, shit-for-brains —

BILLY. Whoa . . . vicious. . .

BOO. Whoa. . . (*Explosive giggling takes over completely. They ram into each other like blocking guards coming off the line. Boo flops down on the bed, Billy stumbles U. near the mirror. The moment begins to pass. Billy straightens up, sees the mirror, makes a face. Boo fidgets a minute. Billy looks at his reflection.*) Hey, Billy. . . Good thing you came to school up here this year. . . (*Billy tries to keep his face blank.*) Last year was — What a drag — (*Nervous laugh.*) Nobody to play with.

BILLY. (*Viciously sarcastic.*) Awww. . .

BOO. Hey, eat it!

BILLY. Eat me —

BOO. — Your mother —

BILLY. Your mother's the shit-shoveller on the Purina Gravy Train. And she eats it every chance she gets —

BOO. (*Yelling; overlapping.*) How much time before dinner, dinkweed? (*On his way to the window, Billy whirls around, and the two of them give each other the finger, fast, like two gun-slingers whipping out their guns. Billy pokes his head out the window, yells.*)

BILLY. HEY, ASSHOLES!! (*Ducks; Boo dives under the bed.*) The clock onna Science Building says twenty to six.

BOO. Twenty minutes! God! I wanted to hear *Highway 61* and the first side. . . (*Billy fakes yawning, going to sleep.*) of *Bringing It All*

Back Home. There's never enough time to do anything in this stupid place! I hate this school —
BILLY. Big deal, who doesn't?
BOO. Every minute you hafta *do* somethin'. Can't stay up late, can't smoke cigarettes, hafta wear ties. It's always *daytime* here.
BILLY. (*Shrugs.*) Stay up all night.
BOO. Sure. They'd kick me right outta here. (*Sudden rage, frustration.*) *God, ya can't even stay up at night!* Aaaaaaaaaaaarrrrrhh!! (*Bitter chant.*) Give us this day our daily hate. . . — Bet Dylan never gets up during the daytime.
BILLY. He's a vampire.
BOO. Be cool to be a vampire. Cooler than this. Get to be invisible.
BILLY. See a lotta free movies.
BOO. Hey. . . I just remembered this dream I had last night.
BILLY. (*Scornful.*) What dream?
BOO. I was at this big posh party in London, at this really rich house. It was really high up, and there were these big picture windows, you could see the river and all the lights of the town. I was with a girl — you know who it was? Trish.
BILLY. That weirdo? What happened, she letcha go all the way or somethin'?
BOO. Nah, we were just lookin' out the window. . . And all these rich little old ladies started runnin' around all over the place, all excited, sayin' Mick Jagger's coming, isn't that wonderful, Mick Jagger's coming. They came up to us and they told us be careful cause the latest thing in London now was sadism, and Mick was really into it. Then they flitted away, laughin' and eatin' *hors d'oeuvres* and stuff, and everybody was just waitin' for Mick to show up. Finally he did, he just walked right in, Marianne Faithfull was with him — she had purple hair. And this whole crowd of little old ladies swarmed all around him. They introduced me to him, and he was incredibly scary-looking, his face, he really made me scared just lookin' at him. He had lipstick on and make-up and he was dressed like a woman, but it was more like he really *was* a woman, a woman and a man at the same time. All of a sudden he started pullin' my hair, really vicious, and he had these bracelets on that were made outta spikes, they jabbed into me, I saw drops of blood drippin' off 'em like a horror movie. I screamed or somethin', I just ran away I was so scared. I ended up in this room away from the party, nobody around, and

31

I saw this guy sittin' on a couch, just sittin' there by himself, really quiet, watchin' TV. I sat down and watched the TV for a couple of minutes, then I turned and looked at the guy . . . and it was Dylan.

BILLY. God. . . I never get anybody like that in mine. All I ever get is all my aunts and uncles and cousins givin' me shit all the time. Always at these big family reunions . . . gross.

BOO. Hey, you wanna stay up all night tonight? It'll be cool, we can take No-Doz. . .

BILLY. Nah. . .

BOO. Nah. . . You never want to do anything.

BILLY. (*Holds up the finger.*) Sit on it and rotate.

BOO. (*Muttering; pacing.*) Aahh. . . Gotta do somethin'. . . (*Suddenly excited.*) Hey! Did I tell you about that song?

BILLY. (*Mocking.*) Oh that song that song!

BOO. Yeah—

BILLY. (*Abrupt.*) What song?

BOO. That song. I told ya. The greatest song I ever heard—

BILLY. —Yeah yeah, there's about thirty of those—

BOO. —Remember? At the concert? Dylan. I told you—

BILLY. —sure sure—

BOO. —Your brain is like Swiss Cheese. —Oh right, I told my roommate.

BILLY. Think I'm brain-damaged. . .

BOO. Friend, roommate, what's the difference—? (*Billy slams a football into Boo's gut, then turns and leans his head against the wall, making jerking-off motions and singing the beginning of the Beatles' "You've Got to Hide Your Love Away,"* changing the lyrics to make it dirty and funny, like "Here I stand, dick in hand" and "beating off on the wall." Boo, overlapping.*) —I heard it at the concert I went to at the end of the summer— Whaddayou doin'? (*Yelling over Billy's singing.*) Shut up! He played this new song, you asshole, it was the first time he ever played it— Hey!

BILLY. (*Belting it like Dylan.*) Hey! Gotta hide your love away!*

BOO. See? Even the Beatles imitate Dylan.

BILLY. The Beatles don't need to imitate nobody, specially Dylan.

BOO. Everybody needs to imitate Dylan.

BILLY. Yeah, you do it enough.

*See Special Note on copyright page

BOO. Whoa . . . vicious. . . (*Dylan voice.*) Got some kinda nerve —

BILLY. — sayin' I'm your friend?

BOO. You just got a lotta nerve, buddy. It's called "Visions of Johanna," it's not on an album yet, but it's greater than anything he ever did —

BILLY. So let's hear it, world's greatest Bob Dylan fan.

BOO. I don't have it, ya jerk, it isn't out yet.

BILLY. So play somethin' else.

BOO. (*Can't believe his ears.*) What? I'm gonna die. *You* wanna hear Dylan?

BILLY. (*Muttered.*) . . .Anything to get you to shut up. . . — Yeah sure, I like Dylan.

BOO. Bullshit.

BILLY. I do. I just like givin' you shit, that's all.

BOO. (*Dubious.*) Okay. How about the flip side of "4th Street"?

BILLY. (*Could care less.*) Sure.

BOO. You're really crackin' up. (*Puts the record on, holding his hands up, signalling for silence, announcing.*) All right: "From a Buick 6." Produced by Bob Johnston, Al Kooper on organ, Michael Bloomfield on guitar.

BILLY. Just play the damn — (*"From a Buick 6" starts, volume way up.* * *Billy shakes his head in disgust. Boo smiles, listens, closes his eyes, bops around.*) Hey! HEY!!

BOO. WHAT?

BILLY. TURN IT DOWN!

BOO. WH — ? NAH!

BILLY. IT'S TOO LOUD!

BOO. I LIKE IT LOUD!

BILLY. I DON'T CARE, TURN IT DOWN!

BOO. BITE THE HAIRY WAZOO! (*Billy goes to the record player, reaches for the volume. Suddenly the lights in the room flicker and go out, and the record player goes off. All the electricity is off. They're totally in the dark.*)

BILLY. Hey! What is this —

BOO. Aw shit. The lights go out right in the middle of Dylan. .

BILLY. Goddammit. Think it's just your room or the whole dorm?

*See Special Note on copyright page

BOO. (*Amused.*) Hey, this is cool.

BILLY. Whaddaya think it is?

BOO. I dunno, but we need two things

BILLY. What?

BOO. Candles and a portable record player.

BILLY. Whaddayou talkin' about?

BOO. I got one over here. Used to be my sister's.

BILLY. Jesus H. Christ.

BOO. Y'wanna hear the song, don'tcha? There's candles in the drawer—

BILLY. Candles? Whaddaya have candles for?

BOO. Just get 'em. I'll get the record player.

BILLY. Candles, portable record player. . . What else ya got, a fallout shelter? (*Gets up cautiously, makes his way across the room, muttering.*) Can't see a damn thing. . . (*Bangs into the bed.*) Ow! Shit. Why am I doing this?

BOO. It's okay, just get your eyes used to it.

BILLY. Yeah, great.

BOO. (*Dylan.*) Don't get hung up on your eyelids.

BILLY. Asshole— (*Billy reaches the desk, opens the drawer and takes out the candles and matches. Boo finds the portable record player.*) Candles. . . weird. . .

BOO. Hey. Billy.

BILLY. What is it now?

BOO. If I can make it over there without touching anything, everything'll be all right for the rest of our lives. Okay?

BILLY. Okay. (*Boo begins moving slowly forward. But Billy lights the candle—*)

BOO. Hey! —Okay, I'll close my eyes. (*He continues across the room, which is a little lighter now. Billy notices something out the window.*)

BILLY. Hey.

BOO. What?

BILLY. C'mere, look at this.

BOO. I gotta do this—

BILLY. Put the record player down, Marston, look at this.

BOO. *What?* (*He opens his eyes, puts it down on the desk, looks out the window with Billy.*)

BILLY. The lights in the Dining Hall aren't on. See?

BOO. God. . .

BILLY. And the Science Building. . . The clock stopped. See? And the Gym. . .

BOO. It's great. Look at that star.

BILLY. Look— All the lights in town are off!

BOO. It's so dark you can see everything.

BILLY. Huh?

BOO. (*Dylan voice.*) Dark into nighttime . . . makin' daytime black. . .

BILLY. Cut the shit willya. Whadda we gonna do?

BOO. (*Dreamy.*) Do?

BILLY. Whadda we gonna do?

BOO. Whaddaya mean?

BILLY. (*Half-kidding.*) It's gotta be the Russians, right?, or the Martians, or whoever it's supposed to be on those Conelrad things.

BOO. Nah, it's the Transylvanians, y'never hear about them any more, they're prob'ly still pissed about Dracula.

BILLY. Shut up. Whaddaya think it is?

BOO. End of the world.

BILLY. Get your radio.

BOO. The transistor?

BILLY. Yeah.

BOO. It's not mine, it's my roommate's, I just borrow it after lights-out.

BILLY. I don't care whose it is, just get it.

BOO. Whaddaya want?

BILLY. *Just get the fuckin' radio, okay?*

BOO. Okay.

BILLY. If we get a station, then we'll know it's just a local thing, okay? (*Boo crosses to his bed and gets the radio from under the pillow. They sit on the bed, the radio in Boo's lap. He fakes turning it on, goes into a Dylan voice.*)

BOO. HOW DOES IT FEEL? (*Billy doesn't laugh, his face set like stone. He grabs the radio from Boo and turns it on. No sound comes out. He turns the dial slowly around, getting nothing. Gets up, paces nervously.*)

BILLY. All the radio stations are off!

BOO. This radio isn't very strong—

BILLY. —The batteries in?—

BOO. —Yeah it's got—

BILLY. —The whole country— It *is* somebody. It's the Russians, for God's sake.

BOO. Russians don't believe in God.

BILLY. What—? Don't be funny, asshole—

35

BOO. Why not—?

BILLY. —Goddamn World War III— (*He turns suddenly and heads for the window, pokes his head out.*) What're those kids doin'? They're chasin' that kid! Hey! WHAT'S GOIN' ON? HEY! YOU GUYS! Jesus Christ, this place's goin' crazy—

BOO. Take it easy, whaddaya tryin' to do, scare the shit outta me?

BILLY. (*Heads for the door.*) I'm goin' out. I gotta find out what's happenin'—

BOO. (*Stopping him.*) Whaddaya nuts? Whaddaya doin'? Don't go out there.

BILLY. Why not?

BOO. I don't know. Just don't. It's stupid.

BILLY. Yeah . . . okay . . . uh. . . What time is it?

BOO. Who gives a shit what time it is? All the clocks stopped.

BILLY. *Hey!* Watch it! I'm tellin' you—

BOO. I'm sorry. Look, the best thing is just stay here, see what happens. Really. C'mon. This is fun.

BILLY. Yeah . . . maybe. . .

BOO. Least we got a record player here. Times like this ya need Dylan. (*He takes "Positively 4th Street" off the electric record player. Billy just watches him, dumb-struck.*) You don't think I'm gonna let myself get blown up without—

BILLY. —You're crazy—

BOO. —a little Dylan.

BILLY. I don't believe this. The world's gonna blow up and you're—

BOO. —Let's play "4th Street" again—

BILLY. —Maybe not the whole world. Just certain parts of America. Like right here. (*Boo opens the portable, puts on the record.*) You can't play that now.

BOO. Why not? (*Billy throws up his hands in disgust, giving up. "Positively 4th Street" starts. * Boo turns the volume way up.*)

BILLY. (*Shouting over the sound.*) You really can't just sit here—

BOO. Sit down, have a good time—

BILLY. We gotta *do* somethin', find out what's goin' on—

BOO. So, Billy, I'll tell ya 'bout that song, that concert—

BILLY. (*Pacing madly.*) *Where is everybody?*

BOO. It was just him the first half, playin' guitar, had his harmonica 'round his neck—

*See Special Note on copyright page

36

BILLY. (*Holding his ears.*) — so fucking *loud!* — (*Turns the volume down.*)

BOO. — played "Love Minus Zero," "Mr. Tambourine Man," stuff like that —

BILLY. *Whaddayou talkin' about?*

BOO. — then he brought out the guys in the band — (*Whips the volume back up high.*) — and a few kids booed, not too many, he looked kinda happy about that —

BILLY. *Shut up!* —

BOO. — I hate all those folk music assholes, music's so much cooler when everything's plugged in —

BILLY. WILL YOU SHUT UP!!

BOO. HEY!

BILLY. QUIT THAT DYLAN SHIT! JESUS! (*Billy yanks the record off. Boo shoves him.*)

BOO. Asshole! (*Billy shoves him back.*)

BILLY. Fuck you! (*Boo lunges for him. They scuffle madly, grappling, arms pumping, flailing wildly. After a minute, they pull away, ready like wrestlers, crouching, feinting.*)

BOO. Leave my records alone!

BILLY. I'm so sick of Dylan —

BOO. I'm so sick of you — (*Boo jumps at him, yelling. They fight each other insanely, in close contact, bashing into furniture, pushing each other all over the room, finally falling on the floor. Billy easily takes Boo, getting him in a vise-like half-nelson, then pushes him away. Boo stays on the floor, Billy gets to his feet.*)

BILLY. Now cut it out! You're really outta your mind!

BOO. (*Bitterly sarcastic.*) Put up your dukes. . .

BILLY. Shut up! Dylan. Whaddaya in love with him? All you ever say —

BOO. (*Scornful, nasty.*) I thought you *liked* him.

BILLY. I just said that to get you to shut up. God — every minute — You're like a girl. (*Boo rises to his feet, singing the last verse of "Positively 4th Street"* as loud as he can, screaming lines like "I wish that for just one time you could stand inside my shoes" and "You'd know what a drag it is to see you" to show his crazed anger. Billy screams to be heard over him, shoving him, belting his shoulder.*) SHUT UP! *SHUT UP!!!!* — What's good about him? He isn't cool, he can't sing. His songs're stupid, they don't make any sense. His voice sucks —

*See Special Note on copyright page

37

(*They're facing each other, screaming simultaneously at the top of their lungs.*)

BILLY. IT SUCKS! BOO. BRAIN-DAMAGED!
SUCKS!! FUCK YOU!
HE SUCKS! YOU SUCK! FUCK YOU!
FUCK YOU!! SHUT UP!! SHUT UP!!

(*Billy reaches the breaking point and hurls Boo head first into the door. A loud bang, and Boo crumples onto the floor, holding his face in pain. Billy backs away, shaking.*)

BILLY. I hate Dylan.

BOO. I hate you.

BILLY. (*Pacing, muttering.*) Jesus, I can't take this shit.

BOO. You can't take anything. You're always so worried about everything—

BILLY. Don't gimme that bullshit—

BOO. You don't like anything— (*An involuntary cry of pain escapes from Boo. He stifles it right away, hiding his face from Billy, who comes over to him.*)

BILLY. (*Scared.*) Are you okay?

BOO. (*Muttered bitterly.*) Put up your dukes. . .

BILLY. Jesus, there's really somethin' wrong with you, Marston, I swear to God—

BOO. There's nothin' wrong with you. . .

BILLY. I never know what you're talkin' about—

BOO. (*Spiteful Dylan voice.*) Your ears're in your back pocket, your eyes're on the ground.

BILLY. (*Gets mad again.*) See? (*Makes a move toward Boo, but stops himself in time. Stalks around the room, muttering, trying to figure things out. Boo stays where he is on the floor, not reacting to him at all, not moving.*) Jesus Christ. . . (*Stops, takes a long look at Boo.*) We just beat each other up over Bob Dylan. (*No response from Boo. Beat. Billy softens a little.*) Hey Boo, I— (*Doesn't know what to say. Takes out a piece of gum, about to offer it to Boo. Doesn't; tosses it aside.*) You wanna try and find out what's goin' on?

BOO. No.

BILLY. (*Voice of reason.*) Don'tcha wanna see what everybody's doin', find out about the lights?

BOO. I like it the way it is.

BILLY. Uh. . . okay. I'm gonna go. You be all right?

BOO. Yeh.

BILLY. I'll try and find somebody, see what's goin' on. Then maybe I'll—come back— Maybe the lights'll go back on.

BOO. Hope not.

BILLY. Okay, guess I'll. . .

BOO. Know what?

BILLY. What?

BOO. I'm the one that's brain-damaged.

BILLY. Take it easy. . .

BOO. I wanted that to happen. I planned it. (*They look at each other a second, look away. Beat.*) I didn't tell you about the song. The guys in the band came out, started playin' electric, really loud, and he was singin'. Never said anything, just stood up there, these blue lights on him, this halo around his hair, it looked like those fires on the edge of the sun.

BILLY. Hey, I'm gonna go—

BOO. Go ahead. (*Billy takes a candle, leaving one on the floor next to Boo. He crosses to the door, opens it.*)

BILLY. Bye. (*Boo doesn't look at him. Billy silently slips away, glancing down the corridor with the light from the candle. Exits.*)

BOO. (*Dylan voice: soft, hoarse.*) You're invisible now. (*Beat.*) See, he wasn't sayin' anything before the songs. But this time he did. He said the next song was a new song, he never did it in front of anybody before, he hoped we liked it. (*Dylan voice: soft, far away.*) Hope ya like it. —And in the song he keeps seein' these visions of Johanna. He's in this motel room with Louise, but these visions keep comin' in. He tries to stop 'em, but they're everyplace he looks, and then his conscience explodes, and the visions take his place, and he just fades away, right in the song, this amazing song, and there's nothin' left 'cept these visions. . . All these visions. . . (*Stops, looks around the room. Looks out the window. Softly sings the opening of "Visions of Johanna," beginning "Ain't it just like the night. . ."* After a couple of lines, he calms down a bit. Picks up the candle.*) Ain't never gonna get light again. (*Blows the candle out.*)

BLACKOUT

*See Special Note on copyright page

SUGGESTED INTERMISSION MUSIC*

"You Baby" — The Turtles
"I Ain't Gonna Eat My Heart Out Anymore" —
    The Young Rascals
"I Fought The Law" — Bobby Fuller Four
"Play With Fire" — The Rolling Stones
"Break On Through" — The Doors

*See Special Note on copyright page

ACT II

1. THINGS WE SAID TODAY

June 1967. 10 P.M.

In the D.R. corner, a lighter is lit and Boo's face is seen, dragging on a cigarette. He's wearing very dark sunglasses, blue jeans, a blue levis jacket and black boots. 18 now, he's more of a loner than before, a little spooky.

The Beatles' "Things We Said Today" plays from a speaker Off Left, where there's a dance going on. *

Lights up: the High School: the corridors and the Teachers' Room. From the dance in the gym Off L., colored lights and music spill out into the corridors and all over the whole stage — primary, vibrant colors, blue, red, purple, green. A twirling/reflecting mirror-ball spins out its thousands of tiny mirror-lights from way Off L.

Boo takes another deep drag off his cigarette. Looks around with furtive suspicious eyes. Hears someone coming from Off L., immediately disappears into the shadows, exiting U.R.

Billy comes in from U.L. He's 18 and laughs nervously more than he used to. He wears a madras jacket, white levis, dark loafers and socks, white shirt, tie. A little drunk, he sings and plays imaginary guitar along with "Things We Said Today." Then sees someone watching him from Off L., gets embarrassed and laughs and waves self-consciously. Leans back against the wall in the corner. Takes out a small bottle of rum from his jacket pocket, swigs a big shot down, pops a piece of gum into his mouth. Stands there listening to the music.

Trish enters from U.R., carrying an unsealed envelope. At 18, she's bloomed: body filled out, face prettier; fuller, less hidden by her hair,

*See Special Note on copyright page

41

which is now longer and more natural. She sometimes covers up her true feelings with easy cynical laughter. Tonight she's dressed up for the dance: mini-dress with bright, vivid colors and designs; sandals, no nylons; a single flower in her hair.

She arrives at the Teachers' Room, stealthily opens the door and turns on the light, gingerly closing it behind her. The room is bare and functional, modern, institutional: gray, white, tan. Nurses' office-type cot against R. wall; large plug-in radio and lamp on table; a row of pigeon-hole letter slots on the Up Right wall.

Trish takes out a letter from the envelope, about to add something to it; reads it aloud bitterly, cynically.

TRISH. Dear Mr. Kelly,
I'm truly sorry my extra credit essay, "The Beatles: The Message in the Music" contained eight run-on sentences, six sentence fragments, excessive use of commas, countless subject/verb disagreements, and improper use of the semicolon. . . Putrid. . . As for your comment that the Beatles' songs are not a suitable subject for composition, may I refer you to Leonard Bernstein's statement in the current issue of *Time* magazine that "The Beatles' melodies are equal to those of Franz Schubert," and to Kenneth Tynan's in the same issue that "The Beatles' lyrics are often reminiscent of T.S. Eliot." And I'm very sorry, no, *distressed*, to learn that in *your* day you weren't allowed to write English essays on the music of Glenn Miller. . . .Whoever *he* was. . .
Yours sincerely,
Patricia Dugan
English 12-B
3rd Period
P.S. May I also remind you that while your subjects and your verbs agree, what you practice and what you preach *don't*. . . You two-faced. . . *(Rushing in from U.L., Peggy opens the Teachers' Room door and comes in. Trish whirls around, scared, grabs her heart. 18 too, Peggy is beginning to lose some of the old confidence. She's dressed for the dance, but differently than Trish: nice red dress, nylons, flats, jewelry, her hair just done, and a little up. She's excited and flighty, like a butterfly; trying just a little too hard to make things work socially, but some of her deadpan*

put-down old self comes through from time to time. "Good Lovin'," the Young Rascals, plays from the dance.) Oh Jesus Christ! . . .

PEGGY. What're you doin' in here?

TRISH. Sendin' a letter to Mr. Kelly. *(Peggy reaches for the letter.)* I wish it was a knife.

PEGGY. "The Beatles: The Message in the Music"? What is this junk?

TRISH. I stopped looking at the pictures and started listening to the words.

PEGGY. Oh God. Who cares? Let me tell you something *really* important. You know who I just saw? Billy.

TRISH. What's he doin' at our school dance?

PEGGY. He didn't even recognize me.

TRISH. How do you know he even saw you?

PEGGY. Cause I know. Could you get him for me? He's over by the water fountain.

TRISH. Get him for you?

PEGGY. Please. . . How do I look? *(Trish rolls her eyeballs, shakes her head, but goes, shoving her letter into Mr. Kelly's pigeon-hole as she does. Outside the Teachers' Room, she looks around Off R., heads that way. Peggy sits and nervously takes out a pocket mirror. Looks at her face. Stops. Discovers something. Stares intently. To her reflection.)* It's a wrinkle. —No it isn't. — Yes it is, what else is it? A crack? —Funny. — They're still crazy about me, right? Crazy about you. Me. You. *(Trish comes back in and locates Billy. He hides his liquor bottle and follows her, paying her a lot of attention.)*

TRISH. Hey. Billy. C'mere.

BILLY. Trish Dugan! . . . I thought that was you. You look . . . nice. *(They go into the room. Peggy puts on a smile, but Billy is too busy admiring Trish to notice her at first.)* Oh. Peggy. Hi. What're you guys doin' in here —? You got a radio —? Hey, we can have a party right here. Hold on a second, I'll be right back. *(He exits, heading Off U.R.)*

PEGGY. A party. We're gonna get kicked out of school the night before graduation for breaking and entering the Teachers' Room.

TRISH. We didn't break in. It wasn't locked.

PEGGY. Great. *(Meanwhile, Boo has reappeared in the D.R. corner, still smoking. Billy spots him, bellows at him like a teacher, as Boo just about has a heart attack.)*

*See Special Note on copyright page

43

BILLY. Okay, buddy, is that a cigarette? (*Cracking up, Billy pulls Boo U. and toward the room.*) Come with me.

BOO. Where?

BILLY. This way. C'mon, you'll like it.

BOO. What?

BILLY. Just come.

BOO. Why? (*As the boys get near the room, Billy takes off Boo's sunglasses, ditches his cigarette. Inside, Boo hangs back, watching, letting Billy run the show.*)

BILLY. You remember Marston, right? Boo? He came by to check out the school.

PEGGY. What'd you come by for?

BILLY. Check out the girls. (*Uncomfortable beat for a second; then Billy hears a song from the dance, Johnny Rivers' "Poor Side of Town," a slow ballad — **) Johnny Rivers! (*Crosses down to Trish, passing Peggy right by. Boo has a mind to ask Trish to dance, but Billy beats him to it. Boo smiles at her. Trish turns away, looks at Peggy, who refuses to look back.*) You wanna dance?

TRISH. In *here*? (*She shrugs why not, and they slow-dance. Boo approaches Peggy and they dance.*)

BILLY. You guys aren't afraid of teachers comin' in?

TRISH. (*Deadpan.*) No, we figured we'd invite 'em in. It's their room. Nyuck-nyuck.

BILLY. Hey, you remember the night we. . .

TRISH. Yeah, I remember. And the next day at school you didn't say a word to me.

BOO. So what're you into now?

PEGGY. What'm I *into*?

BOO. Yeah, you know.

PEGGY. I'm not *into* anything.

BOO. Great. (*Boo dances Peggy over to Billy and Trish. He reaches out and taps Billy on the far shoulder. Billy turns the wrong way, and as he does, Boo fakes one way, moves the other, and ends up in Trish's arms, propelling Billy toward Peggy. Billy slaps Boo on the back. Boo turns and faces him.*)

BILLY. Whaddayou doin'?

BOO. Whaddayou think I'm doin'?

BILLY. I think you're dancin' with the girl I'm dancin' with.

BOO. I think you're right. (*Snarling Dylan voice.*) Hey could you *please* crawl out your window — (*Billy makes a sudden move toward*

*See Special Note on copyright page

44

Boo, who shoves him back, ready to fight, but Peggy steps between them, holding Billy back.)

PEGGY. You'd rather fight than dance with me? *(Embarrassed, Billy turns away, muttering, trying to control his anger, pride on the line. Trish turns on the radio, and the Beatles' "Lucy in the Sky with Diamonds"** blasts out, drowning out the music from the dance.)*

TRISH. *(All excited.)* Beatles' new album! *(She stands in a daze next to the radio, transfixed, eyes closed, body moving to the music. Peggy watches Billy and Boo face each other, as tension mounts.)*

PEGGY. Billy, let's get outta here, okay? *(Relieved, Billy laughs at Boo to shrug off the tension. Boo begins to smile. Billy tosses him a piece of gum as he and Peggy exit, and peace is made. They're out the door and exit U.L. Boo looks at Trish's body from behind, locks the door, tries to break through her cloud.)*

BOO. Hey, uh. . . Trish. . . Hey. . . *(He turns off the radio. Music continues from the dance Off L., faintly: "I'm a Believer," the Monkees.* She looks at him in shock and disbelief. He doesn't know what to say for a second.)* . . .Uh. . . So ya like the Beatles, huh? *(They look at each other warily. Sunglasses on, he slips unconsciously into his Dylan voice and manner.)*

TRISH. You turned it off to tell me that?

BOO. Maybe. . . Only decent album they ever did.

TRISH. *(Amazed.)* You don't like the Beatles?

BOO. Not that much when they first came out. Figured they were just for girls.

TRISH. So whaddaya think I am, one of the guys?

BOO. No. *(Dylan voice.)* You look like a woman, but you break —

TRISH. Who do you think you are? Bob Dylan?

BOO. Maybe. . . So, ya got *Sgt. Pepper's Lonely Hearts Club Band* yet?

TRISH. How could I, it —

BOO. —I only got it cause Dylan hasn't put out anything in so long — since his motorcycle accident —

TRISH. —Wait a minute, you don't have it, it isn't in the store yet.

BOO. I have it. I bought it. Just not around here. You wanna hear it?

TRISH. Where is it?

BOO. Home. — But my parents're there. Yours home?

*See Special Note on copyright page

45

TRISH. They're always home. Why?

BOO. I don't wanna play it with any parents around. If you wanna hear it. . .

TRISH. (*Hesitant.*) . . .I wanna hear it. . .

BOO. . . .Maybe we could go someplace else. . .

TRISH. . . .Maybe. . . (*He takes out his cigarettes, offers her one. She's about to take it—*) Thanks—*Wait a minute this is school I can't smoke here!*

BOO. I got kicked outta my school for smokin.'

TRISH. (*Impressed.*) You got kicked out of school?

BOO. A week before graduation. Billy's a alcoholic and I get kicked out for smokin'.

TRISH. How come you came back here?

BOO. (*Shrugs.*) You want one?

TRISH. *No!* —Yeah. (*She takes one.*) Might as well go all the way— (*Walks right into the cot.*) —I mean, if I'm gonna get in trouble, might as well do it right, right?

BOO. (*Lights her cigarette.*) Might as well. (*He makes a little move to his sunglasses. It makes her jump a little. They both smile at their nervousness, and then he really takes the glasses off. Lights fade in the Teachers' Room and come up on the D.L. area of the corridor where Billy and Peggy are now heading, from U.L. Billy carries a paper cup of Coke, his rum bottle and two straws. Peggy looks back fearfully.*)

PEGGY. That's Mr. Golden! He's givin' us the hairy eyeball!

BILLY. Gimme a break.

PEGGY. He's the worst teacher in the whole school! He's a sadist. I had a dream about once where he was chasin' me down the halls with a waxing machine.

BILLY. Take it easy. If anybody's gonna get in trouble, it's those two, not us.

PEGGY. Why?

BILLY. Cause they're the type. (*Billy mixes the drinks.*) He didn't have to get kicked out of school. He was gunnin' for it all year long. Stupid. I did all kinds of shit and I didn't get kicked out.

PEGGY. Mr. Cool.

BILLY. Damn straight. I beat him up once.

PEGGY. You think you're so tough but you're really just a wimp. (*Tough look from Billy.*) —I'm kidding. But just watch out for Mr. Golden, okay? I don't want to spend the rest of my life in high school. (*Billy nods.*) So why'd you come back here?

BILLY. I dunno. See you.

46

PEGGY. Bull.

BILLY. Hey girl. . . (*They both smile.*) . . .So. How ya been?

PEGGY. (*With an edge.*) Peachy-keen.

BILLY. Peggy Knight — girl most likely to —

PEGGY. — be most likely to. How's everything with you?

BILLY. Everything's great.

PEGGY. Everything's great, huh? How's your love life?

BILLY. Why wouldn't that be great too?

PEGGY. I don't know, why wouldn't it?

BILLY. Drink this. (*He gives her the rum-and-Coke. She takes a big belt, using the straw, coughs and giggles.*) See? You get drunk more if you use a straw.

PEGGY. (*Punches him.*) Tryin' to get me drunk?

BILLY. Sure. (*They both smile. Lights crossfade back to Teachers' Room. Boo and Trish are in the middle of something, finishing their cigarettes. Dance music: "A Thousand Stars," Kathy Young and the Innocents.*)

BOO. (*Dylan.*) — College? That's like the old folks' home.

TRISH. Only college I got into was JC.

BOO. JC? That's for retards —

TRISH. — Thanks a lot —

BOO. — No, you're smart, how'dya —

TRISH. Cause. I got bored doing all those stupid applications, so I made up all these weird answers. Like "List Your Accomplishments"? I wrote that I had the biggest collection of Beatles cards in the entire ninth grade, stuff like that. At JC they can't read, so they took me — (*Sees him laughing.*) — What?

BOO. It's funny.

TRISH. It's gonna be real funny livin' with my mother for the next two years. In two years I'll be *20*. Disgusting. Maybe I should run away from home.

BOO. You should.

TRISH. Close. (*She gets up. He follows her, but she keeps a distance between them.*)

BOO. Why don't ya?

TRISH. You think I meant it?

BOO. Why don'tya just do it? —

TRISH. You can't just do that, you can't just run away from home like when you're a little kid —

BOO. Why not? I ran away from home the day I was born. You ever take drugs?

47

TRISH. Me? I smoked a cigarette dipped in paregoric once. All I got was sick. You ever take drugs?

BOO. No, I 'd really like to though.

TRISH. "No, I'd really like to though." (*Smiling; they're moving closer together.*) Where'd you get a name like Boo anyway?

BOO. Useta liketa scare everybody.

TRISH. I bet. You're weird.

BOO. So're you. (*She smiles, pleased. He takes a breath.*) I followed you home from school once.

TRISH. You did?

BOO. (*Simple: no Dylan inflection.*) In ninth grade. It was the day President Kennedy died. I didn't feel like takin' the bus or anything. I saw you walkin' by yourself. You had a red jacket on. I stayed on the other side of the street and I watched you all the way. The look on your face never changed and you didn't even look up or see me, it made me feel good I don't know why. (*Trying to hide her pleasure, she swallows and turns and walks to the window. He gets a little tougher, a hint of Dylan creeping back.*) If we can get a car, you wanna go down to the Quarry with me?

TRISH. Star light star bright— All the stars are out.

BOO. Million.

TRISH. Thousand.

BOO. Good night for runnin' away.

TRISH. Yeah. . . (*Lights crossfade back to the corridor. From Off L., a song plays: the Beach Boys' "Graduation Day."* Peggy gets all misty, sings along drunkenly with the first verse.*)

BILLY. Hey. What's the matter with you? Gettin' all mushy over some old song about school. You're not the same Peggy I knew way back when.

PEGGY. You're not the same Billy. It's a sad song. Doesn't graduation make you sad?

BILLY. (*Scornful.*) *No!* You kiddin'?

PEGGY. Does it make you scared at all?

BILLY. Scared? Me scared? Hah, what would I be scared of?

PEGGY. Lots of things. . . (*He gets up and moves away from her.*) I'm sorry! Billy, I'm sorry. . . Billy. . . Billy. . .

BILLY. What? I'm not scared. (*He sits down and takes a drink.*)

PEGGY. I know. Billy, are you —don't think bad of me— are you goin' out with anybody now?

*See Special Note on copyright page

BILLY. Yeah— No— I don't know. I was goin' out with this girl up at school. She went to the girls' school in the next town. I guess I'm still goin' out with her, I don't know.
PEGGY. What do you mean?
BILLY. She wants us to go to the same college for four years. Then she wants us to get married and live in the same house and drive the same car and have the same kids.
PEGGY. Is she pretty?
BILLY. Yeah!
PEGGY. What's her name? (*Beat.*) Well, you know what they say about girls that go to private school.
BILLY. Yeah. What? (*Beat.*) She's a weird girl.
PEGGY. Why?
BILLY. Why—? Cause she— Well— (*Wants to tell her but can't.*) She won't let me— She doesn't— I don't wanna talk about it.
PEGGY. Okay. (*Beat.*) What doesn't she do?
BILLY. C'mon. I can't tell a girl.
PEGGY. I know what she doesn't do.
BILLY. What? (*She whispers in his ear. A look of fear appears on his face, but when she moves to look at him, he changes it to a smile.*)
PEGGY. We can go to the Quarry. . .
BILLY. Yeah. . .
PEGGY. Billy. . .
BILLY. Yeah?
PEGGY. I'm so glad it's you. (*He pulls her head to his shoulder so she can't see his face. He strokes her hair, kisses it; with his other hand he reaches for the bottle. She stirs a bit, giggles, puts on a funny/seductive voice.*) Your car or mine? (*Lights crossfade back to Teachers' Room. Dance music from Off L.: "Hang on Sloopy," the McCoys.* Trish is still at the window, Boo getting up his courage—.*)
BOO. You wanna run away with me?
TRISH. Yeah. —What'd you say?
BOO. We're runnin' away. (*Dylan.*) Goin' to Highway 61.
TRISH. Talk like you.
BOO. Go down this fire escape. . .
TRISH. Whaddayou wanna run away for? You're really not gonna go to college?
BOO. Not if we run away.

*See Special Note on copyright page

TRISH. But if you don't, don't they take you in the Army and you have to fight the war?

BOO. How they gonna catch me if we're —

TRISH. (*Flirtatious, ironic.*) What's the matter, don't you care about your country?

BOO. 'Bout as much as it cares for me. (*Giggling, daring, chanting.*) LBJ's a fuckin' A.

TRISH. (*Can't help smiling.*) Sshh —

BOO. Hey, I mean it. Let's go. I really gotta get outta here.

TRISH. What for?

BOO. Plenty of reasons.

TRISH. What reasons?

BOO. (*Dylan voice.*) My head's full of ideas, they're makin' me insane —

TRISH. You always have to be Bob Dylan?

BOO. You always have to listen to the Beatles?

TRISH. I'm a girl, it's different.

BOO. Bullshit, what's different about it?

TRISH. I don't know. (*Flustered; madder and madder.*) Look, I bet I got more reasons to run away than you.

BOO. You think I got kicked out of school cause they caught me? I wanted to. I planned it.

TRISH. So what. I "planned" not gettin' into college —

BOO. Great planning, if you went to college, you'd be away from your mother, you wouldn't have to run away — (*She yells in frustration, belts him on the arm; it brings them closer together.*)

TRISH. Oh God, you think you're so cool? My whole family's crazy. My mother's a maniac. She goes through my drawers. And every night no matter what, if I get home late, she waits up for me, sittin' in the middle of the stairs in the dark just waitin' to scare the shit outta me —

BOO. So? I beat the shit outta my little brother.

TRISH. Big deal! I got a little brother too, you don't think I've ever hit him?

BOO. I didn't just hit him!

TRISH. Whaddaya mean, you didn't just hit him?

BOO. I mean I beat him up!

TRISH. You did not!

BOO. Oh yeah? My parents were downstairs, screamin' at me about school, as usual, so I went upstairs, and *he* started screamin' at me, *my little brother's* givin' me shit about gettin' kicked

50

out of school so I told him to shut up, but he wouldn't, so I started to run at him, but he wouldn't move, so I threw him down on the bed, and I — well, I only hit him twice, but I yelled at them! I ran downstairs and I told 'em *forget about me from now on!* And I ran out of the house and — that's why I came here cause I didn't know where else to go so. . .

TRISH. . . .Oh. . . (*Quieter; their faces almost touching.*)

BOO. . . .I'm glad I did. . .

TRISH. . . .Me too. . .

BOO. . . .That's why I have to run away. . .

TRISH. . . . I stepped on my brother's face once. Not that hard though. (*They kiss: long, deep, passionate, their arms wrapped tightly around each other. Lights cross-fade to the corridor. Peggy's cuddled up to Billy, who takes one last drink out of the straw. Then, courage up, he pulls her head up, moves to kiss her. Just as their lips are about to meet, Peggy hears something Off R. and pulls away. Billy just about falls over.*)

PEGGY. Listen. No more music. The dance's over. We should go — (*Sees something Off R.*) Oh! Billy! Look! It's Mr. Golden! I told you.

BILLY. He can't see us.

PEGGY. We gotta get back to the Teachers' Room and warn Trish — (*All business and action, yanking him up.*) They'll get in trouble —

BILLY. So? (*She punches him in the arm.*) Ow!

PEGGY. Get that bottle! (*He picks it up.*) Hurry! Please — (*Gives him a quick kiss.*)

BILLY. (*Like a kid.*) Peggy. . .

PEGGY. (*Like a Mom.*) Billy. (*She drags him U., luring him with her lips. Corridor lights out. Teachers' Room lights on. Boo and Trish are still kissing. Peggy knocks on the door.*)

TRISH. Peggy.

BOO. Don't say anything. We can stay here.

TRISH. (*Aware of the cot; nervous.*) Uh — I don't know —

PEGGY. Trish.

TRISH. Something's wrong — (*Moves toward the door.*)

PEGGY. — Trish! —

TRISH. (*Turning back to Boo.*) — Are we still running away? —

BOO. — I don't know. I didn't think you'd say yes —

TRISH. — I didn't —

BOO. — Are we still going to the Quarry? —

TRISH. — I don't know —

PEGGY. (*Scared.*) *Trish!*

TRISH. *What?*

BOO. You wanna hear the Beatles' album, don't you? (*Trish hysterically gestures "I don't know," beginning to panic. There's a sound of a crash — glass breaking — outside the door.*)

PEGGY. (*Horrified.*) *Billy!*

TRISH. *What is it?*

BOO. Billy's drunk —

PEGGY. *Trish, open it!* (*Trish opens the door. Peggy and Billy fall inside and close the door behind them, giggling, drunk, giddy.*) Shit.

BILLY. Sorry.

TRISH. What is it? Mr. Golden? (*Peggy nods.*) Aah! —

PEGGY. We're screwed — (*Involuntary giggle.*)

TRISH. Is he gonna come in here?

PEGGY. We'll find out in a minute.

TRISH. Did he see you?

PEGGY. I don't know. I know he heard that bottle break, Billy —

BILLY. Hey —

TRISH. What're we gonna do? — We were gonna run away.

PEGGY. Right.

TRISH. We were.

BOO. We still are —

PEGGY. —Dugan you've really gone off the deep end this time —

BOO. —Aren't we? Trish?

BILLY. What is this shit?

TRISH. (*To herself.*) My ticket to ride. . .

BOO. We'll get a car— (*Aside, Dylan.*) — Should be a motorcycle — Trish? (*She nods yes.*) We'll go down the fire escape. (*Takes her hand.*)

BILLY. (*Cynical; pointing at the door.*) You ain't gonna get very far.

BOO. Oh yeah? (*Boo yanks the plug out of its socket and steals the radio. He and Trish go to the window.*)

PEGGY. How far you gonna go?

TRISH. All the way. (*They start climbing. There's a loud knock on the door. Peggy and Billy are standing there, about to get caught, Trish and Boo get away.*)

BLACKOUT

52

(Running away music: "Midnight Confessions," the Grass Roots. *)

ACT II

2. BIG GIRLS DON'T CRY

Midnight. The Quarry.

Coming up slow on the D.L. area, the lights reveal bushes and branches, a large rock or two on the ground. Dark and scary.

Billy sits on the ground, head down, weary, quiet. Peggy, wearing Billy's madras jacket over her dress, paces back and forth near the car, occasionally lapsing into absentminded versions of her old cheerleader moves.

PEGGY. (*Suddenly, impatiently.*) *Where are they?* (*Billy looks up.*) Billy. (*He chooses to ignore her.*) They didn't really run away—did they? How could they? She doesn't even know him.

BILLY. She wasn't home, was she? Okay, then. (*Gestures with his hands: "No more".*) Want me to turn on the car radio?

PEGGY. No. I don't wanna hear any new songs. "Soldier Boy." I wanna hear "Soldier Boy."

BILLY. They prob'ly won't play it cause it's over a million years old.

PEGGY. "Big Girls Don't Cry." "A Thousand Stars in the Sky" by. . . Kathy Young and the Innocents. How old were we when that came out? Remember Annette?

BILLY. Funicello?

PEGGY. My brother used to love Annette. He and Tommy Tedesco used to watch *The Mouseketeers* on TV every day after football practice so they could watch Annette's tits grow. (*Sighs.*) Now they'll have to settle for Joey Heatherton on USO tours.

BILLY. What're you talkin' about?

PEGGY. They enlisted.

BILLY. In the Army?

PEGGY. Yup. (*Billy gulps. Shivers. Peggy does more cheerleader moves. Billy nervously shuffles a deck of cards.*)

BILLY. You ever come here before? "The Quarry?"
PEGGY. Once. Just once, and I swore I'd never return.
BILLY. Why?
PEGGY. Cause. —God, I'm gonna get in so much trouble—
BILLY. —Jesus—
PEGGY. They prob'ly won't let me graduate tomorrow—
BILLY. —Yes they will, that was just Mr. Golden tryin' to scare ya—
PEGGY. —They prob'ly called my mother—
BILLY. —Peggy!—
PEGGY. —I'm not going home tonight.
BILLY. That's stupid, that's not gonna help.
PEGGY. What do you mean it's not gonna help? Didn't you hear what I just said?
BILLY. If you don't go home, you'll just get in more trouble.
PEGGY. Didn't you hear what I said? You want me to go home.
BILLY. *What?*
PEGGY. Do you?
BILLY. No. I don't want you to go home.
PEGGY. Then why don't you do something about it? —Don't play cards—
BILLY. (*Getting scared.*) —What're you talkin' about—
PEGGY. What do you think? Make me stay.
BILLY. Make you stay. . . ?
PEGGY. (*Fast. Not looking at him.*) I have hated boys for two whole years, and then you show up, and I didn't hate you, so just shut up and make me stay. . . .A thousand stars in the sky big girls don't cry. . . —Oh where *are* they? (*Turns to him.*) Kiss me. (*Closes her eyes. Beat.*)
BILLY. Peggy. . .
PEGGY. Shhh. . .
BILLY. I— I can't. (*She opens her eyes.*) There's something wrong with me.
PEGGY. What?
BILLY. There's— somethin'— wrong with me.
PEGGY. Oh no— (*She cracks up laughing hysterically.*)
BILLY. (*Horrified.*) What's so funny?
PEGGY. (*Giggling even more.*) I've heard that from everybody but never from you.
BILLY. Hey I'm not shittin' around, Peggy! This is serious! (*Hides his face.*)

PEGGY. I didn't mean it! Billy, I'm sorry. . . Billy. . . Billy. . .
BILLY. What?
PEGGY. Tell me about it? Please? You can tell me. . . Honey. . .
BILLY. The girl up at school? She never wanted to, you know,
do it. She said she was afraid it'd hurt cause that's what her
mother told her. The first time you do it it hurts a lot. She said
she hated pain. So I always stopped. Then one night we went as
far as you can without really doing it. It was my birthday. And
she said it was okay, that I could do it, that she loved me so much
she wouldn't mind the pain, she'd make the sacrifice, cause we'd
always be together. (*Shivers.*) It was just the way she said it. I
couldn't do it. I tried. Got scared. No guts. I couldn't do it. So
that's how I know there's something wrong with me. . . I'm. . .
PEGGY. Billy, I wasn't laughing at you. . . (*Little laugh.*) Wait'll I
tell you what's wrong with me. . . (*Touches his face.*) There's
nothing wrong with you. . . (*Softly.*) You think you're so tough
but you're really just. . . (*She gently kisses his face, his eyes, his mouth.
He begins to respond, defrosting, and kisses her back.*)

SLOW FADE TO BLACK

ACT II

3. RUNAWAY

Del Shannon's "Runaway" plays. *

2 A.M. A room at the Paradise Motel. Two beds coming out from the L. wall. Chair at R. wall. Cheap and drab, like a million motel rooms. Outside: darkest night, no stars, strange twisted trees.

Entering from R., Boo crosses the stage, wearing his sunglasses, carrying a laundry bag, a guitar case, a copy of Sgt. Pepper. Opens the door with a key, turns on the light. Strolls into the room, chucks his stuff on the bed. Walks all around, smiling, checking everything out, taking it all in, digging it. Pulls out the Teachers' Room radio from his laundry bag, sets it down near the bed, plugs it in. Stands there looking at the room, his hands beating a nervous rhythm on his legs. Takes the sunglasses off. "Runaway" begins to fade out.

A hand and a suitcase appear at the window, and Trish climbs in, grumbling, stumbling. Boo goes to help her. She gets her balance.

TRISH. I love this room. It's like. . . Study Hall.
BOO. You should've seen the desk guy—
TRISH. —The desk guy just gave it to you? He didn't ask any questions?
BOO. Yeah, but I faked him out. There was this sign on the wall that said "Servicemen Welcome" so I told him I was visiting my father at the Army Base and he couldn't get leave and I had no place else to go, so. . .
TRISH. There's no Army Base around here.
BOO. He believed me. You should've seen this guy. He was bald, he looked just like the guy in *The Tingler*, you know, the one that drives his wife crazy by filling up the bathtub with blood—
TRISH. Shhh— Places like this give me the creeps.

*See Special Note on copyright page

57

BOO. You been to a lot of 'em?

TRISH. No. But did you ever see that movie *Psycho?*

BOO. Yeah. Four times. (*He suddenly does the shower-scene scream and comes after her like Tony Perkins. She screams and runs to the other side of the room. Dylan voice.*) Well whaddaya know, my mind ain't workin', I take a shower, I look just like Tony Perkins.

TRISH. Is there anybody else you like except Bob Dylan?

BOO. Winston Churchill. (*Laughs, jumps exuberantly on the bed. Sunglasses on.*) This is so cool! The Paradise Motel. . . First time I've ever been in a motel, first time I ever stole a car —

TRISH. —Your parents' —

BOO. —First time I ever ran away, first time —

TRISH. You have to keep saying that?

BOO. What? First time? (*Smiles.*)

TRISH. Don't look. (*She goes behind the closet door, taking the suitcase. He waits nervously, trying to be cool. He pulls down the bedspread, finds something on the sheet, flicks it away, arranges things neatly. Then he takes his guitar out of the case, and begins strumming and singing in Bob Dylan style the chorus of "Just Like a Woman."*)

BOO. (*Still strumming, makes the line part of the song.*) . . .Takin' that dress off, huh? . . . (*She comes out, wearing a pair of jeans and a loose-fitting peasant-type blouse, and holding on to her mother's album. He puts the guitar down, takes off the sunglasses and turns to her in anticipation. Disappointed.*) Oh. God what you got in there? You're holdin' it like it was Fort Knox —

TRISH. Nothin'.

BOO. You don't want me to see?

TRISH. If this place is so cool, how come they don't have a TV?

BOO. (*Hurt.*) Whaddaya think we're gonna do, watch TV all night?

TRISH. And the bathroom's down the hall?

BOO. What'd you expect, all the comforts of home?

TRISH. (*At the radio.*) I don't know why you had to steal this. I s'pose you think you're John Dillinger or somebody. . .

BOO. (*Little smile.*) John Dillinger? . . . It's possible. (*He starts prowling around the room; finds the Bible; leafs through it.*)

TRISH. What're you looking for?

BOO. Drugs. I thought somebody left some drugs in it.

*See Special Note on copyright page

58

TRISH. *In the Bible?*

BOO. Maybe a band stayed here. That's where they stay when they're on the road — motels. And that's where they hide their stuff — Bibles. They hollow 'em out — (*Heads for the closet.*)

TRISH. What would a band be doin' around here? Playing at the Army Base? You lookin' for drugs in the closet?

BOO. Found a dime.

TRISH. Great place for a band. I met a guy in a band once. He knew a guy who knew a guy who knew the Beatles —

BOO. (*Sunglasses on; Dylan voice.*) Ooooo, I'm impressed —

TRISH. He told me the original title of "Yesterday" was "Scrambled Eggs." (*She sings a couple of lines of the Beatles' "Yesterday," substituting "Scrambled Eggs" for "Yesterday."** He tries to kiss her; she ducks. She picks up the copy of Sgt. Pepper.*) We can't even play the album. That was dumb, you know, goin' up and gettin' this, you coulda got caught so easy.

BOO. I had to get the car keys, didn't I? What's the difference?

TRISH. The car keys were downstairs and the album was upstairs.

BOO. And my parents were asleep. Big deal.

TRISH. (*Reading the back of the album.*) I read the news today. . .

BOO. (*Sunglasses off.*) You know what was cool? When we first came onto the highway, and seein' it stretch out like that, and then just takin' off. . .

TRISH. Yeah. The lights were nice.

BOO. . . . I kept seein' this vision of the car cracked up, right in the middle of the highway. It was beautiful, kinda. You know, Dylan had this motorcycle accident where he almost got killed —

TRISH. — That means we should do it too —

BOO. — And I kept takin' my hands off the wheel. Closin' my eyes and driftin' like there was some kind of spell on me —

TRISH. Do me a favor, don't let me fall asleep next time I get in a car with you.

BOO. I didn't do anything.

TRISH. Thanks!

BOO. You looked nice asleep.

TRISH. I wasn't just sleeping! You're not the only one who has *visions* and all that stuff!

BOO. No — I know — I —

*See Special Note on copyright page

59

TRISH. I kept seeing myself in this big wheatfield in Kansas. And everything was in black and white. All the people, and the crows. And the Scarecrow kept saying to me, "There's no place like home, there's no place like home." We're not goin' to Kansas, are we?

BOO. Nah. . .

TRISH. Good. We goin' to California?

BOO. I dunno. Maybe.

TRISH. Where *are* we goin'?

BOO. I dunno where we're goin', we're just goin'! Okay? Trust me.

TRISH. Okay, maybe I'll just *go* to my graduation tomorrow.

BOO. What do you mean?

TRISH. I wanna go back.

BOO. We just got here!

TRISH. I don't care. I wanna go home.

BOO. I thought you hated it there.

TRISH. You think I want to live here? You think this is an improvement? (*He stalks around the room, pacing vehemently, ignoring her. She softens, tries to reach him.*) Hey, we don't have to run away.

BOO. Maybe *you* don't.

TRISH. You don't either. Look, our mothers and fathers are still gonna be our mothers and fathers if we run away or not!

BOO. (*Dylan. Sunglasses on.*) Not a chance!

TRISH. *Will you stop it?!* You're just hiding behind that!

BOO. (*Bitter.*) Hidin' from you.

TRISH. (*Quieter; reasonable.*) We can go back. Nobody'll know where we've been.

BOO. (*Anger bursting out.*) I want *everybody* to know where we've been!

TRISH. (*Angry back.*) Yeah if we have a "tragic accident" they'll know, they'll read it in the papers! "Two runaway teenagers killed in fiery crash"—that's what *you* want!—

BOO. That's what happened to James Dean and all those guys, and Dylan almost, I bet he wanted it to—

TRISH. That's the stupidest thing I've ever heard! You think I'm getting into a car with you again, you're crazy! I'd rather call my parents— I'd rather call the police—

BOO. *Police?* We're *criminals* now!—

TRISH. You're not *criminals* cause you steal your parents' car!—

BOO. *Shut up!!* (*She goes and sits on the bed, as far away from him as possible. Tense pause. He paces in small nervous circles. She watches him warily. He stops, looks at her, sits at the foot of the bed, trying to be gentle, taking his sunglasses off.*) Hey, I — (*She quickly takes the pillows from the bed and places them between him and her. Instantly enraged, he grabs them and flings them aside. She flinches and moves further away, cringing against the wall, reaching out and grabbing for her photo album —*) What's in there, your baby pictures? (*— He grabs it, picks it up. She grabs for it, and they struggle. He pulls away with it and looks inside.*) Hey I remember this! —

TRISH. (*Furious; shocked; frightened.*) —What do you mean *you remember this??!!*

BOO. —You had all the Beach Boys songs in it —

TRISH. —You follow me home from school, you go through my drawers, you gonna put *Dragnet* on my trail next? You're worse than my mother!

BOO. (*Flipping through the pages.*) These're all Beatles songs —

TRISH. Give it back!

BOO. What's this? You write this?

TRISH. Don't read that! I don't want anybody to read that —! (*She rushes up to him, but he fends her off.*)

BOO. What is it, your lovebook? Your diary? What'd you write — ?

TRISH. —*None of your business!*

BOO. (*He yanks it away from her, shoves her, holds it over the window as if to throw it out.*) Either I read it or nobody does —!

TRISH. (*Stumbling away; very emotional; feels beaten.*) *Don't!* It's my mother's!

BOO. I thought you hated her!

TRISH. (*Frustrated; confused.*) I— No, I— I wanna go home!

BOO. (*Angry; bitter.*) No place like home!

TRISH. (*Almost crying.*) *I wanna go!* I wanna see my dog. . .

BOO. (*Throws the photo album down.*) We haven't done anything yet!

TRISH. I'll die before I do anything with you!

BOO. (*Dylan voice: vicious, spits it out; sunglasses on.*) You told me — wanted to hold me— You just ain't that strong— (*Trish screams in frustration; yells back at him, her strength returning.*)

TRISH. I read the news today —

BOO. (*Wild insane Dylan; overlapping.*) Anybody can be like me —

TRISH. —A lucky man —made the grade —

61

BOO. — But nobody can be like you — luckily —

TRISH. — Blew his mind — the lights changed —

BOO. — How's it feel — you're on your own —

TRISH. (*Hands over her ears. Screaming.*) — Scrambled Eggs — Love's an easy game to play —

BOO. — No home — A ROLLING STONE!! —

TRISH. (*Chokes back tears of rage.*) STOP IT!! (*She suddenly runs to the door, fumbles with the handle, can't get it open, starts banging on it wildly —*)

BOO. Shut up! You'll wake the whole place up!

TRISH. I'll scream so loud I'll wake the whole world up! (*— He catches her, they struggle, he throws her roughly onto the bed. She scrambles up and stands at the head of the bed, like a cornered animal. He moves toward her to get her to shut up.*) Get away from me! — Don't come near me! — Help! (*Just as she screams, he rushes over and turns on the radio as loud as it can go. The loud instrumental part of the Beatles' "Good Morning Good Morning" blasts out. **) HELP!! I know why you did that — You did that so nobody'll hear me when you —

BOO. What? —

TRISH. — I've seen it in the movies, don't deny it —

BOO. — When I what — ?

TRISH. — *Don't deny it!* —

BOO. — Deny what? — (*He jumps onto the bed. They both stand there, hysterical, screaming at each other over the music.*)

BOO. WHEN I WHAT?	TRISH. DON'T YOU DARE!
DARE WHAT?	SHUT UP! YOU BETTER
WHAT'M I GONNA DO?	NOT —
WHAT? WHEN I WHAT?	I DON'T KNOW!
	I DON'T KNOW! *I DON'T*
	KNOW!

(*He yanks the radio out of its socket and throws it down on the floor with a loud crash. She dissolves into tears.*)

BOO. *Okay? Okay?* (*Still frustrated, he punches the wall, hurting his hand. Stops, turns to her, almost crying.*) What'd you think I was gonna do — ? (*He can't finish; breaks off with a sob; hides his face. She moves closer to him. He lifts his face slowly.*) I don't need any music. (*He kneels on the floor, beginning to break down. She kneels on the bed, getting nearer to him. His sunglasses have fallen off.*)

TRISH. You don't have to be Bob Dylan. You don't have to be anybody.

*See Special Note on copyright page

62

BOO. (*After a beat.*) We'll go home.
TRISH. Home? Never heard of it. (*She pulls him to her and hugs him. Then she gets up and turns off the light in the room. In the shadowy darkness, the Beatles' "Norwegian Wood" begins to play softly.* * *They kiss, and as they fall softly back onto the bed, their kiss grows in desire.*)

SLOW FADE TO BLACK

*See Special Note on copyright page

ACT II

4. GRADUATION DAY

Dawn. The Quarry.

Lights come up very, very slowly. Sounds of birds are in the air.

Peggy lies asleep with her head in Billy's lap. She wakes up and gets up and looks around, hearing the birds, smiling, fascinated with them.

PEGGY. We'll always remember. . . Graduation Day. (*She kisses Billy and he wakes up. They look at each other and smile, happy but shy.*)
BILLY. I was dreaming.
PEGGY. Only two and a half hours to go, Billy. Think I'm ever gonna get out of Martin Van Buren High?
BILLY. Think they'd take me back in?
PEGGY. (*Laughing.*) What?
BILLY. They'd take me back, wouldn't they? I don't want to go to college or anyplace.
PEGGY. What do you mean?
BILLY. The High School. I only went there two years. It was great then, I was the only sophomore on the team, I won that last game for us. They'd take me back. They won't know I went to boarding school. I could just tell 'em my father died or something and we moved away and I had to work for two years to support our family. I just don't wanna *go* anyplace.
PEGGY. Me neither.
BILLY. That's what I was dreaming. You and me could be the King and Queen. We could ride on top of the float.
PEGGY. I'd be Miss Congeniality.
BILLY. You'd be Miss America. Think they'd take us back?
PEGGY. How could they take us back?
BILLY. Do you want them to take us back?
PEGGY. Do I want them —
BILLY. — Yeah.

PEGGY. Do you care?
BILLY. Do you?
PEGGY. Do you?
BILLY. Hey girl. . . (*They kiss. Trish comes in, wearing Boo's sunglasses, carrying the photo album. Boo's right behind her, but hanging back a bit, shy, not quite ready to join the group.*)
PEGGY. Trish! God, I thought something happened to you —
TRISH. It did. (*Flips up her sunglasses. They both smile.*)
PEGGY. You look different.
TRISH. (*Looking at Peggy's stockings, shoes on the ground.*) So do you. (*They hug each other warmly. Billy, watching them, now turns and looks over to Boo. Billy gets up and goes over to him.*)
BILLY. Heard the good news.
BOO. No place like home. (*Billy gives him a playful slap, in their old way. Peggy and Trish are standing with their arms around each other, looking at Trish's photo album.*)
BILLY. Hey Marston, I can remember when you. . .
BOO. Don't remember.
PEGGY. You goin' to graduation?
TRISH. Yeah, soon as I return this to my mother.
PEGGY. Billy, c'mere, look at this.
BILLY. (*Crossing to her.*) What? (*Remembers his cards; gets an idea.*) Hey, sit down a minute, you guys, okay? (*Flashes the cards.*)
PEGGY. Billy. . .
BILLY. C'mon. We got time. (*Billy and Peggy and Trish sit down in a semi-circle at C.*)
PEGGY. "A Thousand Stars!" You still have it!
TRISH. Couldn't erase it.
PEGGY. "I Want to Hold Your Hand —" This is great! (*Billy starts dealing out a hand of cards, but finds his attention turning to the album and Peggy.*)
BILLY. "Twist and Shout," "Boys," — Ed Sullivan! — "She Loves You" — My favorite songs!
TRISH. (*Looks over to Boo.*) "Do You Want To Know a Secret?" Been "A Hard Day's Night." (*Smiling; flirting.*) "I Should Have Known Better —"
BOO. — with a girl like you.
TRISH. "Things We Said Today —"
PEGGY. (*Overlapping Boo and Trish a bit; with Billy.*) "Hold Me Tight," "Baby It's You —"

BILLY. "I Feel Fine," "Thank you Girl—"
PEGGY. "Any Time At All." (*Dissolves into hysterical giggles.*)
TRISH. (*Trying to get Boo to come over.*) Gettin' better all the time. . .
BOO. (*Smiling; moving to her.*) "It's Only Love."
TRISH. I get by— (*Boo joins the others: sits next to Trish and completes the circle.*)
TRISH and BOO. "—With a Little Help From My Friends."
(*The Beatles' "I Should Have Known Better"** plays, beginning to drown out their excited cries of each song title, calling them out simultaneously, overlapping, laughing.*)

PEGGY.	TRISH.	BILLY.	BOO.
"Michelle,"	"She's Leaving	"Drive My	"Ticket to
"Girl,"	Home," "Day	Car," "Run	Ride,"
"Yesterday,"	Tripper," "In	For Your	"Rain," "I'm
"Here, There	My Life,"	Life," "I'm	Looking
and	"Scrambled	Only Sleep-	Through
Everywhere,"	Eggs—" It's	ing."	You."
"Yellow Sub-	true!	"Taxman."	"She Said She
marine."			Said."

SLOW FADE TO BLACK

*See Special Note on copyright page

PROPERTY PLOT

	Onstage	Personal
Act I, Scene 1	2 twin beds (girl's bedspreads)	Billy:
	Upholstered girl's chair	Pack of cards
	Record player	Pack of gum
	Beach Boys albums	
	Assorted 45 rpm records	
	Magazine pictures of Beach Boys on walls	
	Notebooks	
	Trinkets	
	Girl's clothes	
	Toy stuffed animals	
	Photograph album (under bed)	
Act I, Scene 2		Billy:
		Flashlight
		Letter
		Pencil
Act I, Scene 3	Same as Act I, Scene 1, but: (Remove some of the clutter, and replace Beach Boys albums and pictures with Beatles albums and pictures)	
	Princess telephone	
	Transistor radio	
	Photograph of John Lennon	
	Photograph album, pen, ashtray, cigarette pack, matches (under bed)	
Act I, Scene 4	2 twin beds (boy's bedspreads)	Billy:
	Boy's chair	
	Boys' clothes, records, sports equipment	Football
		Pack of gum

	Record player (plugged in) Blanket hung on wall covered with pictures of actresses, Jackie Kennedy, in bathing suits Mirror Record player (portable) Portable radio (under bed pillow) Ashtray Candles, matches (in drawer) Bob Dylan records	
Act II, Scene 1	Cot Table, with plug-in radio and lamp	Boo:
		Lighter Cigarettes Sunglasses
		Billy: Small bottle of "rum" Pack of gum Paper cup of "Coke" and 2 straws
		Trish: Unsealed envelope with letter inside
		Peggy: Pocket mirror
Act II, Scene 2	Bushes, branches, rocks on ground	Billy: Pack of cards
Act II, Scene 3	2 twin beds (Motel) with bedspreads and pillows Motel chair Bible	Boo: Sunglasses Laundry bag, with "clothes" inside Guitar case, with guitar inside *Sgt Pepper* album

Motel key
Plug-in radio (in
laundry bag)

Trish:
Suitcase
Photograph album
(in suitcase)

Act II, Scene 4   Peggy's shoes and stockings   Trish:
(on the ground)   Boo's sunglasses
Photograph album

Billy:
Pack of cards

COSTUME PLOT

PEGGY

Act I, Scene I

Pink blouse
Red/grey plaid skirt
Grey knee socks
Loafers
White half slip
Locket
White undies
Pink hair band
White cotton bra
"P"-ring

Act I, Scene 3

Pink and white
 Polka dot top
Blue shorts
White sneakers
White cotton bra

Act II, Scene I

Blue dress
Strapless bra
White pumps
White purse
Hair up in twist
Hair flower

TRISH

ACT I, Scene I

Orange s. s. blouse
White sweater
Plaid box pleat skirt
White half slip
 scalloped lace

Flowered or pink
 cotton undies
No bra
White socks
Brown suede shoes
Pin
Hair bow

Act I, Scene 3

Red and white striped blouse
White shorts
Red belt
Barrette
Anklette
Flip flops
Bra

Act II, Scene I

Orange striped dress
Orange panty hose
Heels
Bra
Hair ornament

Act II, Scene 3

Orange indian top
Flared jeans
Bra
Orange panty hose
Hair ornament

Act II, Scene 4

Same as 3 but
 no panty hose
No hair ribbon

70

BILLY

Act I, Scene I

Yellow/blue plaid shirt
Chinos
Tee-shirt-white
White jockey shorts
White crew socks
Hi-top sneakers
    with double laces

Act I, Scene 2

Blue camp shirt
Tan cut-offs
Flip flops

Act I, Scene 4

Blue Blazer
Blue oxford cloth
    shirt
Grey/green wool
    pants
Black belt
White socks
White sneakers
Tee-shirt

Act II, Scene I

Madras jacket
2nd blue shirt
Tie
White pants
Brown belt
White socks
Loafers
School ring

BOO

Act I, Scene I

Ochre striped sweater
Olive drab chinos

Mismatched socks
White jockey shorts
Grey hush puppies
Old handkerchief in
    back pocket

Act I, Scene 4

Grey/green striped shirt
White T-shirt
Brown cords
White socks
Brown shoes
Brown belt

Act II, Scene I

Levi jacket
White tee-shirt
Levis
Black boots
Sunglasses

71

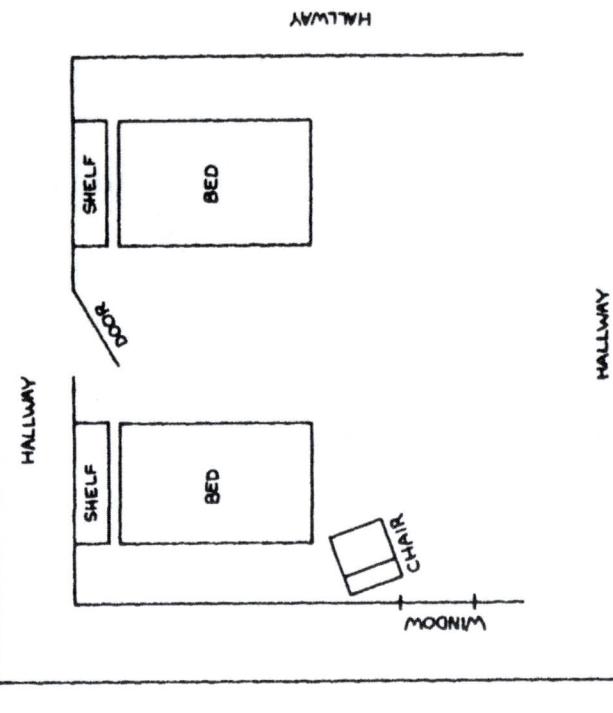

"ALBUM"
SCENE DESIGNS

ACT I

Scene 1: Strip poker & boys' scenes played in the hallway areas. Strip poker opening is down center.

Scene 2: Played in down center area.

Scene 3: Same as Scene 1

Scene 4: Shelves are reversed – and bedspreads are changed to create boys' room.

Walls around room are partitioned, approx. 4 poles on each wall, to give better sight lines. A scrim with star patterns can be lowered for Scene 2.

72

ACT II

Scene 1: Teachers' room/high school Billy & Peggy scenes played on stairs down left.

Scene 2: Scrim w/stairs is lowered and quarry scene is played below.

Scene 3: See other drawing

Scene 4: Billy & Peggy played in front of scrim. Scrim is raised on Boo & Trish entrance. Stage is cleared by this point to give illusion of space & daylight.

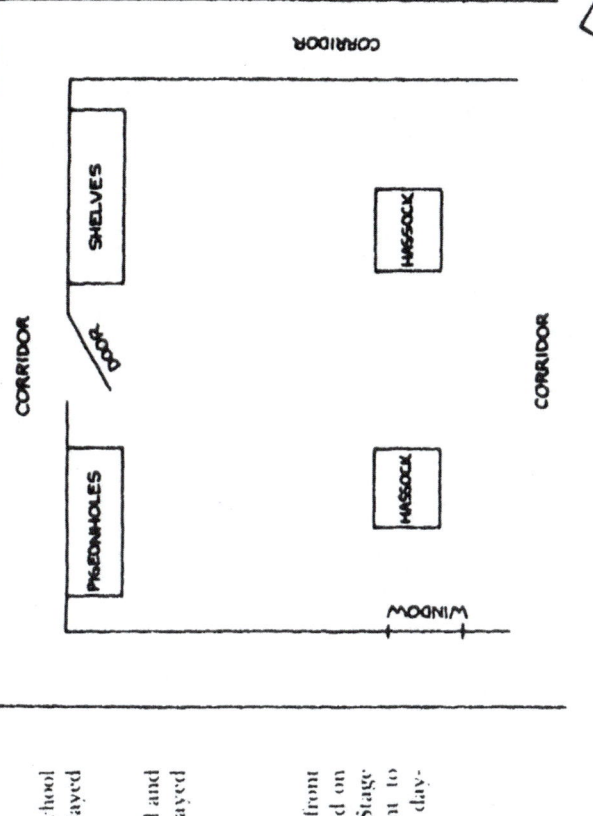

73

ACT II

Scene 3: Motel

SUGGESTED REVISIONS AND DELETIONS
FOR ALTERNATIVE VERSION

Act I, Scene 1

Page 14:
CHANGE:
BOO. . . . Feel up any girl you want.
TO:
BOO. . . . Fool around with any girl you want.

Page 15:
CUT:
BOO. . . . Feel their tits, their legs . . .

Page 17:
CHANGE:
BOO. . . . jeez . . . wish I . . . Oh . . . God . . . gotta get — whoa
. . . give anything for a feel right now . . .
TO:
BOO. . . . jeez . . . wish I . . . Oh . . . gotta get — whoa . . . give
anything for a wet kiss right now . . .

Act I, Scene 2

Page 21:
CHANGE:
BILLY. You incredible dipshit, . . .
TO:
BILLY. You incredible dip, . . .

CHANGE:
BILLY. Bein' a junior counsellor sucks.
TO:
BILLY. Bein' a junior counsellor stinks.

CHANGE:
BILLY. — God, who gives a shit about that? —
TO:
BILLY. — Who cares about that? —

75

CHANGE:
BILLY. . . . we didn't even *hear* the rest of the shit on the album!
TO:
BILLY. . . . we didn't even *hear* the rest of the stuff on the album!

CHANGE:
BILLY. So that's how it is up here, you turd-ball,
TO:
BILLY. So that's how it is up here, you turkey,

Page 22:
CHANGE:
BILLY. You stupid asshole, what the hell you doin' goin' away to school way up in the goddamn woods?
TO:
BILLY. You stupid jerk, what're you doin' goin' away to school way up in the woods?

CHANGE:
BILLY. Sincerely yours, you dipshit, . . .
TO:
BILLY. Sincerely yours, you dip, . . .

CHANGE:
BILLY. What a bunch of shit.
TO:
BILLY. What a bunch of junk.

Act I, Scene 3

Page 23:
CUT:
TRISH. . . . God . . .

Page 24:
CUT:
TRISH. *Shit!*

CHANGE:
PEGGY. —I can't see! God, I can't believe she's gonna do it with him —
TO:
PEGGY. —I can't see! I can't believe she's gonna do it with him —

CHANGE:
TRISH. Oh my God, he's goin' for it already!
TO:
TRISH. He's goin' for it already!

CHANGE:
TRISH. God, you go away for a summer and look what happens.
TO:
TRISH. You go away for a summer and look what happens.

Page 25:
CHANGE:
PEGGY. Oh my God, you got your own phone now?
TO:
PEGGY. You got your own phone now?

CHANGE:
PEGGY. *Dugan!* — God! —
TO:
PEGGY. *Dugan!* —

CHANGE:
TRISH. Bullshit.
TO:
TRISH. Bull.

CHANGE:
TRISH. It gets big? I thought it just, you know, stood up. Like an erection. (*Hesitant pause.*) Do you know, um, do the balls go in with it or do they stay outside?
TO:
TRISH. It gets big? I thought it just, you know, stood up. (*Hesitant pause.*) Do you know, um, do the whachamacallits go in with it or do they stay outside?

Page 27:
CHANGE:
TRISH. You're weird. God, if it changes you this much, I don't know if I wanna do it.
TO:
TRISH. You're weird. If it changes you this much, I don't know if I wanna do it.

CHANGE:
TRISH. God . . .
TO:
TRISH. Wow . . .

CUT FROM:
PEGGY. . . . He kept touching me down there. . . .
ALL THE WAY TO:
. . . He didn't say anything.
AND REPLACE WITH:
PEGGY. . . . The first time it ever felt good like that was way back with Billy.
TRISH. Tell me about now.
PEGGY. That was nice. (*Looks at Trish, who's still anxiously waiting.*) Okay, we're in the back seat, and practically all our clothes are off. And he gets on top of me and starts moanin' and groanin' like he was dyin' or something. Then I feel something touching me and I think, "Okay, okay it's only gonna hurt a second." But it keeps hurting, and nothing's happening. I said, "What's the matter?" And he said, "No, it's okay. It's okay." And he keeps trying and trying and still nothing's happening. He was sweating on me. I felt so squished. I pushed him off me, and he was just sitting there with this stupid look on his face, and I thought, "This is it?" So I said to him, "There's something wrong with one of us." He didn't say anything.

Act I, Scene 4

Page 29:
CUT STAGE DIRECTION:
(*Billy just sits there smiling; the hand behind his head shoots out the finger.*)

Page 30:
CUT:
BOO. Ahh, shit-for-brains—
AND THE NEXT TWO LINES.
AND REPLACE WITH:
BOO. Whoa . . . vicious . . .
BILLY. Whoa . . .

CUT FROM:
BOO. Hey, eat it!
THROUGH:
BILLY. Your mother's the shit-shoveller on the Purina Gravy Train. And she eats it every chance she gets—

CUT STAGE DIRECTION:
(*On his way to the window, Billy whirls around, and the two of them give each other the finger, fast, like two gunslingers whipping out their guns etc.*)

CHANGE:
BILLY. HEY, ASSHOLES!!
TO:
BILLY. HEY, MORONS!!

CHANGE:
BOO. Twenty minutes! God! I wanted to hear . . .
TO:
BOO. Twenty minutes! I wanted to hear . . .

Page 32:
CHANGE:
BILLY. God . . . I never get anybody like that in mine. All I ever get is all my aunts and uncles and cousins givin' me shit all the time. . . .
TO:
BILLY. Wow . . . I never get anybody like that in mine. All I ever get is all my aunts and uncles and cousins givin' me grief all the time. . . .

CUT:
BILLY. (*Holds up the finger.*) Sit on it and rotate.

79

CUT STAGE DIRECTION:
(*Billy slams a football into Boo's gut . . .*
  ALL THE WAY THROUGH:
changing the lyrics to make it dirty and funny, ...
  REPLACE WITH:
(*Billy slams a football into Boo's gut, then sings the Beatles' "You've Got*
to Hide Your Love Away." * *etc.*)

  CHANGE:
BOO. He played this new song, you asshole, it was the first
time he ever played it— *Hey!*
  TO:
BOO: He played this new song, it was the first time he ever
played it— *Hey!*

Page 33:
  CHANGE:
BOO. Bullshit.
  TO:
BOO. Bull.

  CHANGE:
BILLY.   do. I just like givin' you shit, that's all.
  TO:
BILLY. I do. I just like givin' you grief, that's all.

  CHANGE:
BILLY. Just play the damn—
  TO:
BILLY. Just play the record—

  CHANGE:
BOO. Aw shit. The lights go out right in the middle of Dylan.
  TO:
BOO. Aw jeez. The lights go out right in the middle of Dylan.

  CHANGE:
BILLY. Goddammit. Think it's just your room or the whole
dorm?
  TO:
BILLY. Think it's just your room or the whole dorm?

---

*See Special Note on copyright page.

Page 34:
CUT:
BILLY. Jesus H. Christ.

CHANGE:
BILLY. . . . Can't see a damn thing . . . (*Bangs into bed.*) Ow!
Shit. Why am I doing this?
TO:
BILLY. . . . Can't see anything . . . (*Bangs into bed.*) Ow! Why
am I doing this?

CUT:
BILLY. Asshole —

CUT:
BOO. God . . .

Page 35:
CHANGE:
BILLY. Cut the shit willya. Whadda we gonna do?
TO:
BILLY. Cut it out willya. Whadda we gonna do?

CHANGE:
BOO. Nah, it's the Transylvanians, y'never hear about them
any more, they're prob'ly still pissed about Dracula.
TO:
BOO. Nah, it's the Transylvanians, y'never hear about them
any more, they're prob'ly still mad about Dracula.

CHANGE:
BILLY. *Just get the fuckin' radio, okay?*
TO:
BILLY. *Just get the radio, okay?*

CHANGE:
BILLY. What —? Don't be funny, asshole —
TO:
BILLY. What —? Don't be funny —

Page 36:
CHANGE:
BILLY. —Goddamn World War III — . . . .

THROUGH:
Jesus Christ, this place's goin' crazy—
  TO:
BILLY. —World War III—
  THROUGH:
This place's goin' crazy—

  CHANGE:
BOO. Take it easy, whaddaya tryin' to do, scare the shit outta me?
  TO:
BOO. Take it easy, whaddaya tryin' to do, scare the pants offa me?

  CHANGE:
BOO. Who gives a shit what time it is? All the clocks stopped.
  TO:
BOO. Who cares what time it is? All the clocks stopped.

Page 37:
  CHANGE:
BILLY. —so fucking *loud!*—
  TO:
BILLY. —so *loud!*—

  CHANGE:
BOO. —I hate all those folk music assholes,
  TO:
BOO. —I hate all those folk music jerks,

  CUT:
BILLY. QUIT THAT DYLAN SHIT! JESUS!

  CUT:
BOO. Asshole!

  CUT:
BILLY. Fuck you!

  CHANGE:
BILLY. I just said that to get you to shut up. God—every minute— . . .
  THROUGH:
. . . His voice sucks—

TO:
BILLY. I just said that to get you to shut up. Every minute — . . .
THROUGH:
. . . His voice stinks —

Page 38:
CHANGE:
BILLY. IT SUCKS! SUCKS!! HE SUCKS! FUCK YOU!!
SHUT UP!!
TO:
BILLY. IT STINKS! STINKS! HE STINKS! SHUT UP!!

CHANGE:
BOO. BRAIN-DAMAGED! FUCK YOU! YOU SUCK!
FUCK YOU! SHUT UP!!
TO:
BOO. BRAIN-DAMAGED! YOU STINK! SHUT UP!!

CHANGE:
BILLY. Jesus, I can't take this shit.
TO:
BILLY. I can't take this.

CHANGE:
BILLY. Don't gimme that bullshit —
TO:
BILLY. Don't gimme that —

CHANGE:
BILLY. Jesus, there's really somethin' wrong with you,
Marston, I swear to God —
TO:
BILLY. There's really somethin' wrong with you, Marston, I
swear —

CUT:
BILLY. . . . Jesus Christ . . .

Act II, Scene 1

Page 43:
CHANGE:
TRISH. Oh Jesus Christ! . . .

83

TO:
TRISH. Oh! . . .

CHANGE:
PEGGY. Oh God. Who cares? . . .
TO:
PEGGY. Who cares? . . .

Page 46:
CHANGE:
BILLY. . . . Stupid. I did all kinds of shit and I didn't get kicked out.
TO:
BILLY. . . . Stupid. I did all kinds of stuff and I didn't get kicked out.

CHANGE:
BILLY. Damn straight. I beat him up once.
TO:
BILLY. You got it. I beat him up once.

Page 50:
CHANGE:
BOO. LBJ's a fuckin' A.
TO:
BOO. LBJ's a —

CHANGE:
BOO. Bullshit, what's different about it?
TO:
BOO. What's different about it?

CHANGE:
TRISH. . . . sittin' in the middle of the stairs in the dark just waitin' to scare the shit outta me —
TO:
TRISH. . . . sittin' in the middle of the stairs in the dark just waitin' to scare the life outta me —

CHANGE:
BOO. So? I beat the shit outta my little brother.

TO:
BOO. So? I beat up my little brother.

CHANGE:
BOO. . . . *my little brother's* givin' me shit about gettin' kicked out of school. . . .
TO:
BOO. . . . *my little brother's* givin' me grief about gettin' kicked out of school. . . .

Page 52:
  CUT:
PEGGY. . . . Shit.

  CHANGE:
PEGGY. We're screwed— (*Involuntary giggle.*)
  TO:
PEGGY. We've had it —

  CHANGE:
BILLY. What is this shit?
  TO:
BILLY. What is this?

Act II, Scene 2

Page 54:
  CHANGE:
PEGGY. . . . every day after football practice so they could watch Annette's tits grow . . .
  TO:
PEGGY. . . . every day after football practice so they could watch Annette's chest grow . . .

Page 55:
  CHANGE:
PEGGY. Cause. —God, I'm gonna get in so much trouble—
  TO:
PEGGY. Cause. I'm gonna get in so much trouble —

  CUT:
BILLY. —Jesus—

CHANGE:
BILLY. Hey I'm not shittin' around, Peggy! . . .
   TO:
BILLY. Hey I'm not kiddin' around, Peggy! . . .

Act II, Scene 3

Page 58:
   CHANGE:
BOO. . . . Oh. God what you got in there? . . .
   TO:
BOO. . . . Oh. What you got in there?

Act II, Scene 4

Page 65:
   CHANGE:
PEGGY. Trish! God, I thought something happened to you —
   TO:
PEGGY. Trish! I thought something happened to you —

NEW PLAYS

★ **AGES OF THE MOON by Sam Shepard.** Byron and Ames are old friends, reunited by mutual desperation. Over bourbon on ice, they sit, reflect and bicker until fifty years of love, friendship and rivalry are put to the test at the barrel of a gun. "A poignant and honest continuation of themes that have always been present in the work of one of this country's most important dramatists, here reconsidered in the light and shadow of time passed." –NY Times. "Finely wrought…as enjoyable and enlightening as a night spent stargazing." –Talkin' Broadway. [2M] ISBN: 978-0-8222-2462-4

★ **ALL THE WAY by Robert Schenkkan. Winner of the 2014 Tony Award for Best Play.** November, 1963. An assassin's bullet catapults Lyndon Baines Johnson into the presidency. A Shakespearean figure of towering ambition and appetite, this charismatic, conflicted Texan hurls himself into the passage of the Civil Rights Act—a tinderbox issue emblematic of a divided America—even as he campaigns for re-election in his own right, and the recognition he so desperately wants. In Pulitzer Prize and Tony Award–winning Robert Schenkkan's vivid dramatization of LBJ's first year in office, means versus ends plays out on the precipice of modern America. ALL THE WAY is a searing, enthralling exploration of the morality of power. It's not personal, it's just politics. "…action-packed, thoroughly gripping… jaw-dropping political drama." –Variety. "A theatrical coup…nonstop action. The suspense of a first-class thriller." –NY1. [17M, 3W] ISBN: 978-0-8222-3181-3

★ **CHOIR BOY by Tarell Alvin McCraney.** The Charles R. Drew Prep School for Boys is dedicated to the creation of strong, ethical black men. Pharus wants nothing more than to take his rightful place as leader of the school's legendary gospel choir. Can he find his way inside the hallowed halls of this institution if he sings in his own key? "[An] affecting and honest portrait…of a gay youth tentatively beginning to find the courage to let the truth about himself become known." –NY Times. "In his stirring and stylishly told drama, Tarell Alvin McCraney cannily explores race and sexuality and the graces and gravity of history." –NY Daily News. [7M] ISBN: 978-0-8222-3116-5

★ **THE ELECTRIC BABY by Stefanie Zadravec.** When Helen causes a car accident that kills a young man, a group of fractured souls cross paths and connect around a mysterious dying baby who glows like the moon. Folk tales and folklore weave throughout this magical story of sad endings, strange beginnings and the unlikely people that get you from one place to the next. "The imperceptible magic that pervades human existence and the power of myth to assuage sorrow are invoked by the playwright as she entwines the lives of strangers in THE ELECTRIC BABY, a touching drama." –NY Times. "As dazzling as the dialogue is dreamful." –Pittsburgh City Paper. [3M, 3W] ISBN: 978-0-8222-3011-3

DRAMATISTS PLAY SERVICE, INC.
440 Park Avenue South, New York, NY 10016 212-683-8960 Fax 212-213-1539
postmaster@dramatists.com www.dramatists.com

NEW PLAYS

★ **I'LL EAT YOU LAST: A CHAT WITH SUE MENGERS by John Logan.** For more than 20 years, Sue Mengers' clients were the biggest names in show business: Barbra Streisand, Faye Dunaway, Burt Reynolds, Ali MacGraw, Gene Hackman, Cher, Candice Bergen, Ryan O'Neal, Nick Nolte, Mike Nichols, Gore Vidal, Bob Fosse…If her clients were the talk of the town, she was the town, and her dinner parties were the envy of Hollywood. Now, you're invited into her glamorous Beverly Hills home for an evening of dish, dirty secrets and all the inside showbiz details only Sue can tell you. "A delectable soufflé of a solo show…thanks to the buoyant, witty writing of Mr. Logan" –NY Times. "80 irresistible minutes of primo tinseltown dish from a certified master chef." –Hollywood Reporter. [1W] ISBN: 978-0-8222-3079-3

★ **PUNK ROCK by Simon Stephens.** In a private school outside of Manchester, England, a group of highly-articulate seventeen-year-olds flirt and posture their way through the day while preparing for their A-Level mock exams. With hormones raging and minimal adult supervision, the students must prepare for their future — and survive the savagery of high school. Inspired by playwright Simon Stephens' own experiences as a teacher, PUNK ROCK is an honest and unnerving chronicle of contemporary adolescence. "[A] tender, ferocious and frightning play." –NY Times. "[A] muscular little play that starts out funny and ferocious then reveals its compassion by degrees." –Hollywood Reporter. [5M, 3W] ISBN: 978-0-8222-3288-9

★ **THE COUNTRY HOUSE by Donald Margulies.** A brood of famous and longing-to-be-famous creative artists have gathered at their summer home during the Williamstown Theatre Festival. When the weekend takes an unexpected turn, everyone is forced to improvise, inciting a series of simmering jealousies, romantic outbursts, and passionate soul-searching. Both witty and compelling, THE COUNTRY HOUSE provides a piercing look at a family of performers coming to terms with the roles they play in each other's lives. "A valentine to the artists of the stage." –NY Times. "Remarkably candid and funny." –Variety. [3M, 3W] ISBN: 978-0-8222-3274-2

★ **OUR LADY OF KIBEHO by Katori Hall.** Based on real events, OUR LADY OF KIBEHO is an exploration of faith, doubt, and the power and consequences of both. In 1981, a village girl in Rwanda claims to see the Virgin Mary. Ostracized by her schoolmates and labeled disturbed, everyone refuses to believe, until impossible happenings appear again and again. Skepticism gives way to fear, and then to belief, causing upheaval in the school community and beyond. "Transfixing." –NY Times. "Hall's passionate play renews belief in what theater can do." –Time Out [7M, 8W, 1 boy] ISBN: 978-0-8222-3301-5

DRAMATISTS PLAY SERVICE, INC.
440 Park Avenue South, New York, NY 10016 212-683-8960 Fax 212-213-1539
postmaster@dramatists.com www.dramatists.com

NEW PLAYS

★ **ACT ONE by James Lapine.** Growing up in an impoverished Bronx family and forced to drop out of school at age thirteen, Moss Hart dreamed of joining the glamorous world of the theater. Hart's famous memoir *Act One* plots his unlikely collaboration with the legendary playwright George S. Kaufman and his arrival on Broadway. Tony Award-winning writer and director James Lapine has adapted Act One for the stage, creating a funny, heartbreaking and suspenseful celebration of a playwright and his work. "…brims contagiously with the ineffable, irrational and irrefutable passion for that endangered religion called the Theater." –NY Times. "…wrought with abundant skill and empathy." –Time Out. [8M, 4W] ISBN: 978-0-8222-3217-9

★ **THE VEIL by Conor McPherson.** May 1822, rural Ireland. The defrocked Reverend Berkeley arrives at the crumbling former glory of Mount Prospect House to accompany a young woman to England. Seventeen-year-old Hannah is to be married off to a marquis in order to resolve the debts of her mother's estate. However, compelled by the strange voices that haunt his beautiful young charge and a fascination with the psychic current that pervades the house, Berkeley proposes a séance, the consequences of which are catastrophic. "…an effective mixture of dark comedy and suspense." –Telegraph (London). "A cracking fireside tale of haunting and decay." –Times (London). [3M, 5W] ISBN: 978-0-8222-3313-8

★ **AN OCTOROON by Branden Jacobs-Jenkins. Winner of the 2014 OBIE Award for Best New American Play.** Judge Peyton is dead and his plantation Terrebonne is in financial ruins. Peyton's handsome nephew George arrives as heir apparent and quickly falls in love with Zoe, a beautiful octoroon. But the evil overseer M'Closky has other plans—for both Terrebonne and Zoe. In 1859, a famous Irishman wrote this play about slavery in America. Now an American tries to write his own. "AN OCTOROON invites us to laugh loudly and easily at how naïve the old stereotypes now seem, until nothing seems funny at all." –NY Times [10M, 5W] ISBN: 978-0-8222-3226-1

★ **IVANOV translated and adapted by Curt Columbus.** In this fascinating early work by Anton Chekhov, we see the union of humor and pathos that would become his trademark. A restless man, Nicholai Ivanov struggles to dig himself out of debt and out of provincial boredom. When the local doctor, Lvov, informs Ivanov that his wife Anna is dying and accuses him of worsening her condition with his foul moods, Ivanov is sent into a downward spiral of depression and ennui. He soon finds himself drawn to a beautiful young woman, Sasha, full of hope and energy. Finding himself stuck between a romantic young mistress and his ailing wife, Ivanov falls deeper into crisis, heading toward inevitable tragedy. [8M, 8W] ISBN: 978-0-8222-3155-4

DRAMATISTS PLAY SERVICE, INC.
440 Park Avenue South, New York, NY 10016 212-683-8960 Fax 212-213-1539
postmaster@dramatists.com www.dramatists.com

NEW PLAYS

★ **MOTHERS AND SONS by Terrence McNally.** At turns funny and powerful, MOTHERS AND SONS portrays a woman who pays an unexpected visit to the New York apartment of her late son's partner, who is now married to another man and has a young son. Challenged to face how society has changed around her, generations collide as she revisits the past and begins to see the life her son might have led. "A resonant elegy for a ravaged generation." –NY Times. "A moving reflection on a changed America." –Chicago Tribune. [2M, 1W, 1 boy] ISBN: 978-0-8222-3183-7

★ **THE HEIR APPARENT by David Ives, adapted from Le Légataire Universel by Jean-François Regnard.** Paris, 1708. Eraste, a worthy though penniless young man, is in love with the fair Isabelle, but her forbidding mother, Madame Argante, will only let the two marry if Eraste can show he will inherit the estate of his rich but miserly Uncle Geronte. Unfortunately, old Geronte has also fallen for the fair Isabelle, and plans to marry her this very day and leave her everything in his will—separating the two young lovers forever. Eraste's wily servant Crispin jumps in, getting a couple of meddling relatives disinherited by impersonating them (one, a brash American, the other a French female country cousin)—only to have the old man kick off before his will is made! In a brilliant stroke, Crispin then impersonates the old man, dictating a will favorable to his master (and Crispin himself, of course)—only to find that rich Uncle Geronte isn't dead at all and is more than ever ready to marry Isabelle! The multiple strands of the plot are unraveled to great comic effect in the streaming rhyming couplets of French classical comedy, and everyone lives happily, and richly, ever after. [4M, 3W] ISBN: 978-0-8222-2808-0

★ **HANDLE WITH CARE by Jason Odell Williams.** Circumstances both hilarious and tragic bring together a young Israeli woman, who has little command of English, and a young American man, who has little command of romance. Is their inevitable love an accident…or is it destiny, generations in the making? "A hilarious and heartwarming romantic comedy." –NY Times. "Hilariously funny! Utterly charming, fearlessly adorable and a tiny bit magical." –Naples News. [2M, 2W] ISBN: 978-0-8222-3138-7

★ **LAST GAS by John Cariani.** Nat Paradis is a Red Sox-loving part-time dad who manages Paradis' Last Convenient Store, the last convenient place to get gas—or anything—before the Canadian border to the north and the North Maine Woods to the west. When an old flame returns to town, Nat gets a chance to rekindle a romance he gave up on years ago. But sparks fly as he's forced to choose between new love and old. "Peppered with poignant characters [and] sharp writing." –Portland Phoenix. "Very funny and surprisingly thought-provoking." –Portland Press Herald. [4M, 3W] ISBN: 978-0-8222-3232-2

DRAMATISTS PLAY SERVICE, INC.
440 Park Avenue South, New York, NY 10016 212-683-8960 Fax 212-213-1539
postmaster@dramatists.com www.dramatists.com